# OBJEC

A book series about the hidden lives of ordinary things.

*Series Editors*:

Ian Bogost and Christopher Schaberg

*Advisory Board*:

Sara Ahmed, Jane Bennett, Johanna Drucker, Raiford Guins, Graham Harman, renée hoogland, Pam Houston, Eileen Joy, Douglas Kahn, Daniel Miller, Esther Milne, Timothy Morton, Nigel Thrift, Kathleen Stewart, Rob Walker, Michele White.

In association with

LOYOLA UNIVERSITY NEW ORLEANS    Georgia Tech | Center for Media Studies

## BOOKS IN THE SERIES

*Driver's License* by Meredith Castile

*Golf Ball* by Harry Brown

*Drone* by Adam Rothstein

*Hotel* by Joanna Walsh (forthcoming)

*Refrigerator* by Jonathan Rees (forthcoming)

*Shipping Container* by Craig Martin (forthcoming)

*Silence* by John Biguenet (forthcoming)

*Phone Booth* by Ariana Kelly (forthcoming)

*Glass* by John Garrison (forthcoming)

*Waste* by Brian Thill (forthcoming)

*Tree* by Matthew Battles (forthcoming)

*Hair* by Scott Lowe (forthcoming)

*Dust* by Michael Marder (forthcoming)

*Doorknob* by Thomas Mical (forthcoming)

*Blanket* by Kara Thompson (forthcoming)

# remote control

## CAETLIN BENSON-ALLOTT

Bloomsbury Academic
An imprint of Bloomsbury Publishing Inc

B L O O M S B U R Y
NEW YORK • LONDON • NEW DELHI • SYDNEY

**Bloomsbury Academic**
An imprint of Bloomsbury Publishing Inc

| | |
|---|---|
| 1385 Broadway | 50 Bedford Square |
| New York | London |
| NY 10018 | WC1B 3DP |
| USA | UK |

**www.bloomsbury.com**

**BLOOMSBURY and the Diana logo are trademarks of
Bloomsbury Publishing Plc**

First published 2015

**Library of Congress Cataloging-in-Publication Data**
Benson-Allott, Caetlin Anne.
Remote control/Caetlin Benson-Allott.
pages cm. – (Object lessons)
Includes bibliographical references and index.
ISBN 978-1-62356-997-6 (hardback: alk. paper) –
ISBN 978-1-62356-311-0 (pbk.: alk. paper) –
ISBN 978-1-62892-345-2 (ePDF) – ISBN 978-1-62892-344-5 (ePub)
1. Television–Channel selectors–History. 2. Television viewers–Psychology.
3. Grazing (Television) 4. Television–Social aspects.
5. Popular culture–United States. I. Title.
TK6655.C5B46 2015
302.23'45–dc23
2014033295

ISBN: PB: 978-1-6235-6311-0
ePub: 978-1-6289-2344-5
ePDF: 978-1-6289-2345-2

Series: Object Lessons

Typeset by Deanta Global Publishing Services, Chennai, India
Printed and bound in the United States of America

To John Benson, with love

# CONTENTS

List of Illustrations  viii
Acknowledgments  x
Introduction  xi

**1**  Changing volume and values  1

**2**  Convenience, necessity, nuisance  43

**3**  It's complicated  87

Afterword  125
Notes  130
Index  147

# LIST OF ILLUSTRATIONS

1 1929 advertisement for Kolster K-45 radio receiver 2

2 A homebuilt spherical audion radio receiver
circa 1915 7

3 1932 advertisement for Stromberg-Carlson
Telektor radio-phonograph 13

4 General Motors Radio Company's 281
radio converter "remote control" 15

5 1933 advertisement for Philco Lazy-X radio receiver 17

6 Illustration from "Radio Aims at Remote Control"
(*Popular Science Monthly*, November 1930) 28

7 1938 advertisement for the Philco Mystery Control 31

8 Image from a 1951 flier for Zenith's Lazy Bones
remote control 36

9 A 1955 Zenith Flash-Matic "flash gun" remote control 48

10 1955 advertisement for Zenith Flash-Matic
television set with "flash gun" 50–1

11  1956 advertisement for Zenith Space Command 200 remote control    55

12  1961 advertisement for Admiral Son-R remote control    57

13  1960 advertisement for Zenith Space Command 400 remote control    63

14  1957 advertisement for Zenith Space Command 400 remote control    65

15  Frame grab from RCA Victor's "Television Remote Control (Tuner)" (circa 1961)    71

16  A remote control for a Jerrold set-top cable converter box, circa 1975    75

17  1980 advertisement for Sony Betamax "Time Commander" remote control    78

18  A 1990 Sony RM-K1T remote control    91

19  RCA's 1983 Digital Command Center and 1984 Dimensia Digital Control remote controls    95

20  A 1985 CL9 CORE remote control    102

21  A 1990 Mitsubishi PRM-1 remote control    109

22  US patent application illustration for Doug Patton's Palm-Mate remote control    110

23  A 2008 Universal Electronic Atlas UCAP universal remote control    115

24  A 2009 second-generation Apple Remote    121

# ACKNOWLEDGMENTS

This book would not have been possible without the invaluable contributions of my research assistants: Anne Jefferson, Katharine McCain, and Brett Treacy. Neda Atanasoski, Ian Bogost, Jacob Brogan, Ashley Cohen, Amelie Hastie, Brian Hochman, Carla Marcantonio, Jeff Menne, Joan Perlow, Seth Perlow, Nicole Rizzuto, Christopher Schaberg, and Daniel Shore all provided feedback and sage counsel. Haaris Naqvi and Bloomsbury Press deserve great praise for their expeditious professionalism. I am also grateful for the intellectual and financial support of Georgetown University's English Department, its incredible faculty and staff.

Finally, I want to thank friends and family too numerous to list here and express my undying gratitude to my father, who taught me to appreciate the art of design.

# INTRODUCTION

The remote control for my DIRECTV digital video recorder has forty-five buttons; the television remote has forty-four and the Blu-ray controller forty-nine. The Apple TV remote only has seven buttons, but the iHome stereo remote has seventeen. That's a total of five remotes and 162 remote-control buttons in my living room alone. There are more remotes in the kitchen, the bedroom, and even the car. Yes, my new car stereo came with a remote control, for reasons that have everything to do with the social history of this peculiar device and nothing to do with practical necessity. These reasons are hard to recognize because the remote control's very pervasiveness obscures its history. When remotes are everywhere, they don't seem to come from anywhere in particular. Yet there was a first remote control and a first use of the term "remote control." Uncovering these origins and the remote's subsequent evolution will reveal how it became the most common media device of the twenty-first century.

Remote control is both a technology and a cultural fantasy. Remotes are the dominant interface for communicating with media electronics today, but "remote control" is also an historically specific idea about how audiences might interact with the mass media, how they might maintain control as the media occupied ever more time in their lives and space in their homes. In 1929, advertisers represented the first remote controls for radio receivers as luxury items, in order to make radio listening seem more sophisticated and appealing to high-income audiences. In the 1950s, as television upended American domestic routines, TV manufacturers promoted the remote control as a tool to help men maintain sovereignty over the new electronic guest in their homes. Thirty years later, advertisers tied infrared remote controls to the 1980s ideal of personal empowerment and social advancement through high-tech electronics.

At each juncture, advertisers characterized remote controls as cutting edge; they ignored the device's history in order to propagate new ideas about what a remote control could signify. But remote control design is always historically and culturally contingent. People—inventors, industrial engineers, and entrepreneurs—developed and adapted remote control technology at specific moments in response to specific cultural pressures and market forces. Of course the remotes themselves did not always live up to their hype. Because remotes are designed to manage electronic devices, they quietly encourage us to use more—and buy more—electronics. They seem indispensable because they perpetuate the problems they purport to solve. That's why they often feel like a convenience and a nuisance at the same time.

Remotes are cultural artifacts, objects that contain significant information about the societies they emerge from and impact. They have a lot to teach us, for instance, about changes in US gender roles and family dynamics during the twentieth century. They reflect the ways that broadcast media's presence in the home challenges longstanding ideas about what counts as masculine and feminine, public and private, within and beyond our control. Just as we program media devices with our remotes, remotes program us to interact with the media in specific ways. Their design invents, invites, and encourages behavior such as muting commercials and fast-forwarding through sexually explicit scenes. So it would be a mistake to think that remotes do not produce profound changes in their environments. Cultural artifacts are not just passive registers of social forces; they are also social forces in their own right.

In fact the term *remote control* began as a meditation on social forces, on the strengths and shortcomings of democracy. The term originated in England in the eighteenth century, during the 1794 trial of Thomas Hardy for high treason. Hardy was one of twelve political organizers persecuted by the British Parliament, which feared that their calls for electoral reform might inspire an uprising similar to the French Revolution. During Hardy's trial, Solicitor General Sir John Milford coined the phrase "remote control" to describe the "control of people or institutions exercised at a distance."[1] He contrasts "remote control" with Hardy's dream of direct democracy, of "a revolutionary government based on the rights of man, and equal citizenship, and so on, in which the people are to be considered as constantly sovereign, as constantly exerting the sovereign authority, and as having perpetual control over the whole government of the country; not an indirect and *remote control*."[2] For Milford, "remote control" describes a representative democracy in which people elect delegates to govern on their behalf. Milford opposes "remote control" to Hardy's philosophy of direct democracy, but Hardy's dream lives on in our use of remote controls today. Their design—their many buttons and multifunction capabilities—encourages us to believe that remotes actually communicate our choices and preferences to the media. Remotes give us push-button sovereignty, but they also limit that sovereignty to our personal television sets. You can fast-forward all you want, in other words, but the media is not going to stop using commercials anytime soon.

Politicians and political theorists still use "remote control" in its civic sense, but the term attained its modern definition—as "a device for controlling a piece of equipment at a distance"—in the early twentieth century. The remote control device was born when Nikola Tesla sensationally launched the world's first remote-controlled boat at the 1898 Electrical Exhibition in New York City.[3] Tesla, an electrical engineer and one of the original inventors of radio communications, described his invention as an "apparatus for controlling from a distance the operation of the propelling engines, the steering apparatus, and other mechanism carried by moving bodies or floating vessels."[4]

In those days, there was much more military than commercial interest in remote control technology. At the same 1898 exhibition where Tesla introduced his remote-controlled boat, another radio pioneer, Guglielmo Marconi, presented a wireless detonation system for use in the Spanish-American War.[5] André Gabet patented a radio-controlled torpedo in France in 1909, just in time for the First World War. During the war itself, British and German military forces experimented with remote-controlled rockets, tanks, planes, and boats.[6] The most successful of these experiments was the German FL-7 or *fernlenkboote* (remote steering boat), which seemed directly inspired by Tesla's radio-controlled boat.[7] The FL-7s were unmanned watercrafts that could carry up to 1,500 pounds of explosives and were connected to on-shore steering stations via fifty-mile spools of wire. They functioned like torpedoes rather than vessels, because their operators simply ran them into enemy targets to initiate devastating explosions. First deployed in 1916, FL-7s created a precedent for modern military drones, although we rarely describe such devices as remote-controlled today.

It is worth noting that Tesla's patent for his radio-controlled boat never uses the term "remote control." Engineers didn't refer to electronics as remote controlled until Walter V. Ash introduced the term in his 1903 patent for an "apparatus for remote control of electric motors."[8] Ash was the first American to use the term "remote control" to patent one device that controlled another from a distance. His patent led the way for an adjective (remote) and a nominalization (control) to become one compound noun: remote control. This is a small syntactical shift, but it's important, because it explains some key ideological distinctions between remote control and other kinds of controllers.

For instance, the "remote" of "remote control" stresses the space between the user and the machine, a space that the remote control also occupies in a peculiar way. Remote controls use intangible signals—electronic pulses, radio waves, ultrasonic tones or light waves—to convey information across a physical interval. Both electric power and radio waves were new technologies in the early twentieth century, and together with the spread of telegraphy, they were changing the way people understood the world and the very notion of space. As various storywriters, poets, and journalists attest, the air seemed suddenly alive with information in ways it never had before. Electronic media were transforming space into ether, a medium for communiqués from great distances, including the great beyond.[9] Home radio receivers brought remote voices indoors, making them a part of private family life. Such incursions disrupted the remoteness of the home, the family's psychic distance from the wider world. The material world was no longer providing firm boundaries for the psychic world, a phenomenon that generated both excitement and anxiety for radio listeners. In short, radios and electronic communication were forcing an ideological crisis for many early-twentieth-century families. Remote controls promised to restore the family's control over its remoteness, and best of all, Father would not even have to get up from his easy chair to use it.

Such control can feel empowering, but let's remember that "control" is not synonymous with "power." A remote control helps us mute commercials, but it cannot actually stop those commercials, because remote controls do not give their users power. Power is an ability to change the world around you; it is not defined by preexisting parameters, as is control. A person exercises control within a specific arena, but power exceeds the individual acts of control that it enables. Control requires a complementary object: the thing one has control of or over. That complement can be implied—for example, she's in control (of the whole department)—but it still exists. Power can take a complement but does not require one, because English speakers have absolutized and hypostatized power differently, more thoroughly than control. So, for instance, a 1950s remote control user might have control over four possible volume levels: low, medium, high, and mute. He had that choice. But the person who had the power was the one who designed the remote, the one who established those four options.

Of course, remote controls do not emphasize the difference between power and control—that would hardly be good for business. The modern universal remote control, for instance, appears to bestow a lot of power on its user. It seems like you ought to be able to do just about anything with a device that has that many buttons, when in fact all its possible functions have been predetermined by a team of product designers and engineers. Those designers also know that the more buttons a remote control has, the fewer we actually use.[10] In other words—and since its invention—the user's lack of power is intrinsic to the remote control device. We tacitly acknowledge this limit when we refer to these devices as "remotes." The term "remote" focuses our attention on the glories of remote-ness, the pleasure of tuning a television set without getting out of the easy chair. In so doing, it helps us overlook the failed promise of "control."

Not so with controllers for video games and model vehicles. Although these devices resemble and even share some functions with remote controls, the colloquial term *controller* attests their significant difference as cultural artifacts. Controllers direct devices that go somewhere, either physically (in the case of model boats, planes and cars) or virtually (in the case of video games). The term "controller" can also refer to a person—she who commands or regulates—so it reflects the model vehicle driver or video game player's identification with the device.[11] A controller is an extension of the person using it, but a remote control is not. Instead its name connotes a very specific historical battle over controlling or being controlled by the mass media. As a culture, then, we have reserved the name *remote control* for those gadgets that express our dreams and anxieties about how we relate to radio, television, and other audio-visual media.

*Remote Control* tells the story of these gadgets in order to explore how objects participate in and complicate the relationship of American consumers to mass media broadcasters and electronics manufacturers. Its three chapters focus on three pivotal phases in the design of remote control devices when such tensions changed media technology and were changed by it. Chapter 1, "Changing volumes and values," focuses on the introduction of wired radio and television remotes in the late 1920s and early 1950s, respectively. At first, ads for these devices presented them as luxury items, but later they used ideals of familial harmony and domestic sovereignty to propose remotes as tools to battle noisy commercials—in short (and ingeniously), to peddle one media device as the solution for another. Chapter 2, "Convenience, necessity, nuisance," looks at the ways that wireless ultrasonic and infrared television remote controls encouraged people to erroneously equate choice with power. As they grew in popularity between 1955 and 1985, wireless remotes were part of a wider television culture that changed domestic life in America, creating new habits like *channel surfing*, which made changing the channel seem like active engagement with the media. Chapter 3, "It's complicated," analyzes how "universal" remotes and branded remotes (e.g., the Apple Remote) were supposed to solve the problem of remote control clutter. Unfortunately, they replaced clutter with confusion, which led to a fad for simplified secondary remotes, which led to more clutter. Manufacturers claim that these multifunction remotes all offer us control over excessively complicated home entertainment systems, but in fact they only exacerbate the problem they are supposed to solve, leaving us mired in clutter and confusion. Finally, the conclusion argues that product design is an important and understudied component of media history. We do not just watch television shows and movies; we watch them through devices whose material forms, limitations, and advantages affect how we view our world.

# 1 CHANGING VOLUME AND VALUES

"I tell you it was absolutely uncanny."[1] So begins a 1929 print advertisement for Kolster's K-45 radio receiver, the first radio receiver to come with a remote control. In this ad, an anonymous narrator tells the story of his initial encounter with remote control (see figure 1). "'Shall we have some music?'" the anonymous narrator suggests to his fictional host. "'Surely,' answered Mr. Jackson. But instead of walking 'way round into the library—he turned to an interesting device on the table beside him—*and pressed a button.*"[2] The incredulous narrator is shocked and delighted by the miraculous little box his friend employs, but the scenario he describes hints at changes far more significant than just a novel gadget. Over the past five years, broadcast radio had effected a cultural revolution in the United States: the first infiltration of broadcast media into the home. During this turning point in telecommunications, when the amateur "wireless" culture was giving way to a more homogenized broadcast "radio" culture, manufacturers began to add remote controls

**FIGURE 1** "Absolutely uncanny": A 1929 advertisement for Kolster's K-45 radio receiver with remote control.

to their radio receivers. At first, they hope that attaching remote controls to some of their top-of-the-line receivers would entice affluent consumers who might previously have considered it a lower class or 'mass' entertainment. Later on, manufacturers also promoted remote controls to middle-class consumers as tools for policing irritating commercial interruptions.

The remotes themselves did not always live up to adver-tisers' promises, of course, and they changed radio culture in ways neither manufacturers nor listeners could have pre-dicted. Yet their advertising and design—not to mention their use, the way Americans integrated remotes into their households—stabilized our concept of "remote control" and set important precedents for television and future consumer electronics remotes. History has mostly forgotten radio remotes, but they established the paradigm for remote con-trol that shapes our experience of home media today.

Kolster's first remote control did not come cheap; the company asked about $500 for a K-45 with remote in a year when the median price for radio receivers was around $139. Adjusting for inflation, this means that Kolster was charging nearly $7,000 for a reasonably nice but hardly extraordinary radio that happened to have an extra set of tuning dials on a box attached via a twenty-foot cable. No wonder Kolster's early ads for the K-45 pictured men in tuxedos and women in evening dresses; only upper-class individuals could afford such devices. Kolster wanted its consumers to imagine remote controls as indulgences, as evidence of their wealth and power. That's why the K-45 receiver also resembled a beautiful piece of furniture, a "richly grained walnut cabinet—unique and exquisite in appearance" that belonged in an upper-crust library or living room.[3] It is prominently featured in the ad's illustration while the remote itself is discretely hidden on a side table. It blends right into its elegant environment, and in so doing, also helps the radio receiver shake off its unseemly technological past to become the civilized entertainment medium of the future.

Kolster is using these associations to imagine a whole future for radio: radio as a fit pastime for sophisticated, cosmopolitan adults. Their ad evokes radio's new urbane appeal as a broadcast medium and suggests that remote controls will be indispensable luxuries for upper-class radio fans. Kolster's ad reveals that remote control is part of the story of how radio was integrated into American domestic spaces and routines—which means it is also part of the story of how radio paved the way for television, cable boxes, computers, and other mass media technologies to get inside our houses.

Over the course of the next three decades, manufacturers developed remote controls as a concept and a technology, and advertisers refined their approach to fusing remote controls with middle-class domestic traditions. With help from the burgeoning field of radio journalism, they successfully coopted and stabilized the concept of remote control. After all, "remote control" had no fixed meaning in 1929. At that time, other industries still used the phrase to refer to in-wall light switches and automatic hood releases.[4] Radio marketing campaigns defined the remote control as a secondary tuning station and associated it with wealth and privilege. In the decades to come, they would expand that association to draw in even more potential consumers, sacrificing aristocratic pretension to emphasize middle-class family values. Ads of the 1930s heralded remotes as devices of personal empowerment in a war to protect the home from commercial invaders—although their actual design encouraged users to listen to more consumer radio and at higher volumes than before. This early conflict between cultural fantasies of remote control and the devices themselves continues to shape how we think about and use remote controls today. That's why it's almost impossible to understand how we interact with media technology without understanding the history of remote control.

*     *     *

Radio receiver remotes encouraged audiences to sit back and enjoy commercial broadcasts, but radio was not always synonymous with broadcasting. Before the Radio Act of 1927, all sorts of individuals and businesses experimented with "wireless telegraphy." In the 1910s, wireless culture was largely associated with amateur "ham" radio operators. Using homebuilt receivers and transmitters, wireless enthusiasts could talk to or listen in on other amateur hobbyists, political organizations, local corporations, and a few early broadcast chains. As of 1917, almost nine thousand Americans had radio broadcasting licenses and exchanged information across a homebuilt telecommunications network.[5] Most were using equipment they assembled from kits or by following instructions in new magazines like *Radio Age* and *Popular Mechanics*.

Building a radio required a lot of technical knowledge and skill, and as a result, radio entered American culture as a highly specialized and highly gendered hobby. Because the scientific knowledge and labor associated with building and operating one's own radio were considered masculine, most early wireless aficionados were male. Newspaper and magazine articles also portrayed radio as a messy hobby that men and boys should restrict to rooms where women rarely ventured, such as the workshop, the basement, the attic, and the garage. To be fair, many homemakers wanted "the wireless" exiled to a male ghetto. Early radios were an unsettling mess of wires and tubes completely at odds with early twentieth-century home décor. Worse yet, many were powered by portable batteries whose acid could ruin furniture and carpets (see figure 2).

Radio patent-holders like the Radio Corporation of America (RCA) wanted to change that impression and sell more radios. To achieve that goal, they needed to change the culture of wireless, to make it more commercial and more family friendly. Thus radio manufacturers started to sponsor entertaining and edifying broadcast programming, specifically the kind of entertainment and educational programming they believed that bourgeois consumers would

**FIGURE 2** A refurbished antique homemade radio receiver.

enjoy. It was a marketing strategy akin to "if you play it, they will buy." In 1926, RCA launched the first radio network, the National Broadcasting Company (NBC). NBC played high quality musical, dramatic and educational programming designed to appeal to a middle-class family audience. They wanted to combat the mass medium's early reputation as a lower-class entertainment in order to attract more affluent listeners, listeners that would enable them to charge larger sponsorship fees.

At the same time, RCA and its competitors began to manufacturing new radio consoles that were "family friendly," meaning compatible with conventional American interior design. Like gramophone producers before them, they encased radio receivers in cabinets that could blend in with classic furniture styles. Put simply, they made new media look old fashioned to appeal to traditional consumers. With these strategies, radio manufacturers distanced themselves from the mysterious, male-dominated world of wireless and the mess associated with homebuilt radios. Many of their ads even implicitly characterized amateur wireless culture as dangerous or deviant by emphasizing the virtues of stylish factory-built radio receivers instead.

Such ads were intended to make radio seem more physically and morally attractive to homemakers, the women who managed and decorated the house. During the nineteenth century, the Victorian doctrine of "separate spheres" designated the home as "women's territory" and its moral and physical upkeep as "women's work." This ideology—which had roots in the political philosophy of Aristotle—drew strong and gendered distinctions between the public sphere and the private sphere: the public was male, the private female. The family home was supposed to be a retreat for men from the stress of work and politics, so women were morally and religiously obligated to maintain it as a safe, nurturing environment for their husbands and children. Never mind that around 20 percent of women worked outside of the home in the first decades of the twentieth century, as did many children.[6] Ideologies are based on ideals, not realities. But even when the separation of spheres was not as rigid as its rhetoric suggested, electronic media still posed a challenge to the ideal of a domestic sanctuary. How were women supposed to maintain the privacy of the home when outside voices could intrude at any moment? 1920s radio manufacturers had to resolve this social quandary. The remote control would offer one solution, but the problem itself was also mitigated by a growing trend in domestic architecture, namely the living room.

In the early twentieth century, American culture was in the process of reinterpreting the home as a shared space for family leisure. Electricity and household electronics created more time for recreation and brought new forms of recreation into the home, including radio. While only 8 percent of US households were wired for electricity in 1907, nearly 70 percent were by 1930, and electric light and wiring dramatically changed how people were able to use and enjoy their houses.[7] For instance, houses built for electricity and collective family leisure tended to feature so-called living rooms instead of formal parlors. The living room was understood as a gathering place where the family could relax or entertain together.[8] Living rooms had been part of Western architecture since the late seventeenth century, when French architect Charles Augustin d'Aviler "drew a distinction between formal display spaces and a new kind of room, spaces that were 'less grand.'"[9] But while eighteenth- and nineteenth-century living rooms might have felt less grand, they were still not a place to unwind after work. During the early twentieth century, grand rooms and parlors gave way to living rooms, but that meant that modern living rooms needed to serve two functions: to provide space for family leisure and to function as a display space for family prosperity. If radio manufacturers wanted to get their products into such spaces, they needed to satisfy both demands. They needed to make machines the entire family could use and show off— not just fathers and sons.

It can be difficult to imagine this kind of complex socio-technological engineering today, but Christine Frederick chronicled radio's design shift for the popular magazine *Wireless Age*. Writing in 1925 she observed, "Until this current year radio was the toy and the joy of men rather than women. It has only been since women have taken a practical home making interest in radio" that manufacturers started to make "higher class, more beautiful and more artistically designed sets." According to writers like Frederick, women's first concern regarding radio ought to be aesthetic; they should embrace "artistically designed sets" that echoed traditional US furniture design.[10] Radio manufacturer Atwater Kent echoed Frederick's philosophy with ads that assured readers that "radio needn't disturb any room."[11] These ads tended to run in women's magazines like *Ladies' Home Journal*. They sold radios as furniture rather than technology and as continuations rather than interruptions of design traditions in order to make radio seem compatible with traditional family values.

Unfortunately, radios were challenging family values aurally as well as visually. In order to sell radios to family audiences, manufacturers started to equip them with loudspeakers so everyone could hear. Most homebuilt wireless receivers used headphones because they did not have the capacity to amplify weak signals. Headphones worked well when Junior wanted to play with the ham radio alone in his bedroom, but they were extremely inconvenient for a family of four trying to listen to a variety show together. Adding loudspeakers had a tremendous effect on radio sales, but it presented serious problems for the ideology of the private sphere. Once radios had loudspeakers, their noise went everywhere, drowning out competing conversations. Sound waves aren't unsightly like batteries and wires, but you also can't hide them behind a pretty wood façade. Like radio itself, amplified sound threatened the boundary between public and private, family life and the outside world, because it gave outside voices the power to shout crass commercial messages or political tirades directly into the living room.

To make loudspeakers less threatening, to help families avoid the messages they didn't want to hear, manufacturers needed to make radios easier to tune. Early radio receivers required elaborate tuning rituals with multiple dials. As late as 1930, *The Canadian Magazine* still referred to radio's tuning interface as "a multiplicity of knobs which was bewildering to the uninitiated." [12] In truth, the first commercially produced radio receivers were no more user-friendly than homemade wireless sets had been. It was not until 1926 that "technical controls had been simplified down to two knobs (tuning and volume) so that practical know-how was no longer needed."[13] Ads for this new generation of radios trumpeted their simplified interfaces as well as their powerful loudspeakers and detailed wood cabinetry. They often featured women at the controls to demonstrate just how attractive, easy to use, and family-friendly radio could be. Female models served as eye candy for male consumers, but they also showed how manufacturers were shifting cultural perceptions. With a woman at the dial, radio was no longer just a boy's toy. It had become a family device, and the scene was set for remote control.

*    *    *

By 1929, manufacturers hoped that radio's reputation had shifted far enough that some consumers were willing to spend more money for the luxury of tuning their high-end receivers from their armchairs. Early ads for radio remote controls emphasize the ways that these accessories can improve radio's integration into readers' lives and living rooms. Recall Kolster's 1929 ad for the K-45, in which men and women make a black-tie evening out of listening to the radio. The remote control is nearly hidden on a side table, yet the narrator still enthuses over its breathtaking powers. None of the characters in the illustration are looking at it, yet the remote control's powers determine the scene. A similar dynamic is at work in Stromberg-Carlson's 1932 ad for the Telektor radio-phonograph with remote control (see figure 3). In the ad's illustration, the hostess of a formal tea party reaches for her Telektor remote as her guest looks on in admiration.[14] The remote is located near the center of the tea table, a place of prominence that connects remote control

FIGURE 3 "All completely controlled by Telektor": A 1932 advertisement for the Stromberg-Carlson Telektor radio-phonograph.

with the new ideology of *conspicuous consumption*. Coined by Thorstein Veblen in 1899, *conspicuous consumption* described a growing social trend among the upper-middle class to display their wealth and power through material acquisitions. During the twentieth century, sociologists and social commentators expanded Veblen's concept to include a broader habit of spending discretionary income on luxury items rather than practical needs, especially luxury items that consumers count on others to recognize as luxury items (think Christian Louboutin high heels and their signature red soles). The Stromberg-Carlson ad applies this logic to remote control. Its illustration implies that purchasing a remote-controlled radio-phonograph will earn the attention and admiration of your friends and houseguests. Just leave the remote out on your tea table, the ad suggests, and watch them coo with jealousy.

The Telektor remote itself complicates its ad's rhetoric of conspicuous consumption and emphasis on social display. Its casing is so unadorned as to be unsightly, almost as unsightly as an old wireless set. Most early radio receiver remotes were rather plain, especially compared to the consoles they accompanied. The K-45 remote was a simple metal box with ten buttons and a volume knob. While it featured some decorative scrollwork, it also bore a thick brown cord. The Telektor was even worse. Fully ten inches long, it possessed two rows of labeled buttons and none of Kolster's subtle ornamentation. Compare these utilitarian devices with the elaborate inlay and engraving in contemporaneous radio cabinets, and it's easy to see that Kolster and Stromberg-Carlson intended their remotes to be *in*conspicuous. Remote control should be visible, that is, but not the remote controls themselves.

To that end, many 1930s radio manufacturers disguised their radio receiver remotes to look like other objects. The General Motors Radio Company, for instance, hid its 281 remote inside a standing ashtray (see figure 4). Launched in 1931, the 281 was technically a radio converter but General Motors marketed it as a remote control. Converters were basically super-charged antennas that a buyer could attach to his or her existing radio receiver to improve weak signals, which the converter would transform into an intermediate

**FIGURE 4** The General Motors Radio Company's 281 radio converter "remote control." Photo used by permission of John Kusching, Radio Museum, www.radiomuseum.org.

frequency and deliver to the receiver via antenna wire. The 281 improved on existing converter design by adding tuning and volume control knobs (not to mention an ashtray). But in as much as it disguised its technical functioning, the 281 complicates Veblen's notion of conspicuous consumption. After all, how can the inconspicuous also be conspicuous? The answer is novelty. The ashtray-cum-remote-control begs to be revealed as more than what it seems. It disguises its nature in order to make the final revelation that much more impressive. Moreover, its novelty as a dual-function object enhances the novelty of remote control. In fact, this principle also explains the almost anti-ornamental design of Kolster and Stromberg-Carlson's remote controls: their unassuming exteriors only made their powers that much more impressive once revealed.

The 281 was one of many early remote controls camouflaged as furniture rather than housed in a tabletop device. Take Philco's first remote control, the Lazy-X, which doubled as an ornate Queen Anne side table. With its lid down, the Lazy-X was indistinguishable from any other side table, but in fact it contained a secret radio receiver. Like the 281, then, the Lazy-X was not technically a remote control; rather, it was the radio. The console cabinet it came with only contained loudspeakers. So in effect—and rather ingeniously—Philco made a remote control by taking the radio out of its cabinet radio and moving it into a separate piece of furniture.

Regardless, ads for the Lazy-X employed the language of remote control in order to emphasize the luxury of side-table tuning. "Sink deep into your most comfortable chair," one ad commanded, as "a radio of glorious tone begins playing across the room. ... That's Lazy-X convenience, made possible by Philco Perfected Remote Control!"[15] Philco's vision of remote control differs considerably from its predecessors', however. Unlike the earlier Kolster and Stromberg-Carlson campaigns, Philco's Lazy-X ad pictures and explicitly solicits a middle-class consumer (see figure 5). It emphasizes comfort to convince readers that this new feature—remote control— can ease radio's integration into an average US household. It also implies that changing the station is the major hurdle to most people's radio pleasure. Philco promised that the Lazy-X would make radio so pleasurable that "almost automatically Lazy-X doubles the number of stations you hear and enjoy— by doubling the ease with which you change the dial setting."

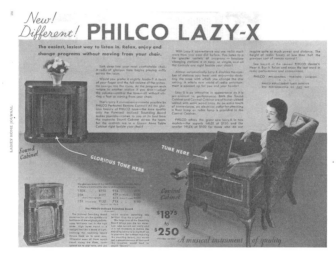

**FIGURE 5** "Sink deep into your most comfortable chair": A 1933 advertisement for Philco's Lazy-X radio receiver with remote control.

By that logic, remote control can resolve almost any problem in radioland, including a lack of radio stations, and even when it's not really a remote control.

Philco's first remote control ad concludes by guaranteeing that with a Lazy-X, "a whole new world of radio entertainment is opened up for you and your family." This final line evokes the excitement of early wireless culture and associates it with the safety of broadcast and its promise of family-friendly domestic entertainment. But neither this "you"—presumably the *pater familias*—nor his grateful family appears in Philco's illustration. Instead it depicts a woman reclining alone next to her Lazy-X. The model rests one hand regally on the arm of her wingback chair while the other reaches beneath a hinged panel in the top of the Lazy-X. Her grace and femininity mark the Lazy-X as both opulent and approachable, while her jewelry, make-up and high heels suggest that remote control radio befits an upper-middle-class lifestyle. Or perhaps I should say upwardly mobile lifestyle, because the Lazy-X was not especially expensive. In 1933, it cost as little as $100, yet Philco marketed it as a luxury item for the masses. With "the height of radio luxury at less than half the previous cost of remote control," the Lazy-X contributed to the commercialization of the American Dream, our illusion that we can be happy purchasing the outward signs of the good life (as opposed to working our way toward a better life). Advertisers promise that as long as their readers continue to equate the good life with material acquisition, they can buy rather than work their way to it. With the

Lazy-X, Philco suggested that remote control is one way to purchase a superior lifestyle.

*        *        *

Philco was one of the first radio manufacturers to sell its remote controls through images of feminine repose, but the technique thereafter became an industrial trend. Many Lazy-X ads depict a woman alone with her remote-control radio, reclining in her armchair and tuning her device with just the smallest movement of her hand. These images of ladylike elegance were not necessarily aimed at the female viewer, however. Such ads appeared in family journals like *The Saturday Evening Post* that were likely to have male and female readers. Advertisers needed to appeal to the men in financial control of most US households during this period. Female models could elicit male desire as well as—perhaps even more than—female identification. They helped male and female readers imagine domestic life as a full-service world in which ladies have ample time to relax with their favorite radio programs and gentlemen need do no more than lift a finger to have their needs met. They encouraged both sexes to imagine the home as a space of luxury and relaxation— although sometimes a total lack of models could entice male readers equally well. One Lazy-X ad bucks the female model trend by leaving its armchair empty, as if waiting for the reader to take a seat. A magazine lies open across that seat, perhaps a copy of the very same *Saturday Evening Post* in which that ad appeared.[16] Atop the Lazy-X side table, a cigar smolders languidly in an ashtray. Someone has had to step away from the remote—why? Whatever for? The only thing missing from this fantasy of upper-crust tranquility is someone to take up that cigar, sit back with the magazine, and tune in to his favorite station. Perhaps that person should be you.

Introducing gender roles into remote control advertising was rhetorically complicated for electronics manufacturers during the 1930s, though, because of the lingering influence of the separate spheres doctrine. While ads needed to appeal to men as the financial heads of their households, (even though women were in charge of the shopping), men were also responsible for protecting their families from the corrupting influence of the outside world that radio threatened to bring into the home. Meanwhile female readers needed to be encouraged to embrace radio as aesthetically pleasing, easy to use, and beneficial to the family. These competing demands would shape the rhetoric around remote control for decades to come, but in the case of 1930s remote control advertising, it is sufficient to note how the comely female model resolves many of these issues. As a potential mother, she marks the radio as family friendly, but her body also offers visual pleasure for male viewers. Through her embrace of the technology, she naturalizes the radio's presence in the living room. Her light touch on the remote control implies that buyers won't have to worry about maintaining control over the mass media. Her presence suggests that radio technology can be exciting, attractive, and socially conservative all at the same time.

But gender wasn't the only ideology manufacturers used to sell radio remotes. Class differences also provided significant fodder for advertisers. In 1931, there was a brief craze for radio receivers disguised to look like grandfather clocks. Manufacturers were capitalizing on the aristocratic connotations of the grandfather clock to reach a new group of consumers, namely middle-income and working-class urban dwellers. The Westinghouse Electric and Manufacturing Company cashed in on this trend with the Columaire radio and its optional remote control. "Tired of the commonplace?" one Columaire ad asked. "Haven't you wished you could own a radio that didn't *look* like every other one on the street?"[17] By casually mentioning "the street," Westinghouse implicitly aimed their appeal at apartment dwellers. Their ad boasted that the Columaire "takes only one square foot of floor space," so it can fit "in the corner of even the smallest of small rooms." Westinghouse never explains why you'd need a remote control in "even the smallest of small rooms," but then remote control was never about physical necessity. It represents the new values of consumer culture, where purchasing power equals social power, even personal identity. Westinghouse plays up this point by using black-tie parties as settings in other Columaire ads, milieus that also allow it to disavow, or at least disguise, its address to lower-middle-class consumers. After all, no one wants to be hailed as poor, especially not by an advertisement that's trying to sell you something. With the Columaire, Westinghouse affirmed remote control could be—should be—part of everyone's class aspirations. Remote control would bring luxury to your home regardless of your social stature.

Inevitably, the actual Columaire remote was nowhere near as majestic as its ads implied, but it was typical of 1930s remote control design trends. About the size and shape of "a two-pound chocolate box," it featured a rectangular grid of buttons for tuning to preset stations, raising and lowering volume, and turning the radio on or off.[18] *Popular Science* ran a profile of radio receiver remotes in 1934 that suggested that most were similarly utilitarian in design: large boxes of push buttons connected to their radio consoles by wide ribbon cables. A few had visual tuning meters, but for the most part, 1930s radio remotes exhibited none of the flair or visual appeal of contemporaneous receivers.[19] Those radio remotes not disguised as household objects tended to expose their technological nature; in fact, their mechanical efficiency had a lot in common with early wireless equipment. Both eschewed decoration and celebrated the technological even if it put them at odds with tradional home décor.

Many early remotes actively disrupted domestic aesthetics and routines. All of the remotes mentioned thus far had to be connected to their receivers via fifteen- to thirty-foot cords. Some tuned their receivers by activating small motors attached to the console's tuning dials while other delivered electrical impulses directly to the receiver itself, but all needed cables to deliver their signals. Homeowners had to run these cables under carpets and along baseboards to avoid tripping over them. As a result, the first remote controls provided only *remote*, as opposed to *portable*, control. While the Telektor ad suggests that its hostess takes her remote with her wherever she entertains, in fact most wire remote controls were stationary. Once the 281's power and antenna cords had been secured, for instance, the unit itself could not be moved. Nor was it designed to be, given that it was, after all, a full-size metal ashstand filled with radio tubes. But remote control cables didn't just determine the location of remote controls. They also affected the placement of the radio cabinet, rugs, side tables, and even other electrical appliances in the room. If your sofa was more than fifteen feet from the radio, or if you didn't have an adequate side table to support your new remote control, then you'd be forced to start moving furniture. Some luxury! Through their cords and inconveniences, remote controls subtly asserted the media's control over radio culture, including the living room.

*    *    *

Remote controls hinted at the growing power of the mass media, but they were marketed as a means to limit that power. As commercial radio became a stronger cultural force during the 1930s, remote controls were increasingly advertised as devices to keep that force, well, under control. The 1930s manufacturers promised that their remotes would help listeners to lower the volume on irritating commercials, to tune away from shrill pitches and flagrant appeals. Thus began the second phase in remote control marketing, when advertisers stopped promoting remotes as luxurious novelties and started advocating their ability to protect families from the commercialism of broadcast radio. In a beautiful twist of logic, advertisers urged consumers to buy a commodity (the remote control) in order to curb the presence of commodity culture in their homes.

Radio was not the first media technology to bring commercial entertainment into private residences, but it was the first to introduce advertisements that consumers could not skip or overlook (e.g., newspapers and magazines). Phonograph recordings already brought home audiences prerecorded music, vaudeville acts, and other performances, but because listeners paid for these records, few contained overt advertisements.[20] Since radio was free to listeners, it required a different business model. As early as 1916, David Sarnoff—the future president of RCA—imagined the "radio music box" becoming a household utility that would provide listeners with free music and programming by charging advertisers to sponsor the programs. Sarnoff predicted that, "Aside from the profit to be derived from this proposition, the possibilities for advertising for the company are tremendous, for its name would ultimately be brought into the household."[21] That sacred private sphere would be breached in the name of business. It's worth noting that for Sarnoff, radio's broadcast potential and commercial potential are inextricably linked. There was no broadcast radio that didn't rely on advertisements, not for him and not for the United States. With the exception of a few early education stations, Sarnoff's vision continues to dominate US radio.[22]

But it creates a confusing dynamic among broadcasters, advertisers, and listeners because it means that the business of American radio is selling audiences to advertisers. Pop songs, radio programs, even the traffic report; they're bait to catch our attention so that advertisers can pitch their wares.

By the early 1920s, radio audiences had already begun to resent broadcast advertisements. They regarded commercials as interruptions, which led to animosity toward programmers and sponsors. As early as June 1922, an editorial in *Radio Digest* complained bitterly about radio programs peppered with sponsor messages. "Do you wish to tune up your receiving set and sit back to take in a good concert or listen to something interesting and instructive and get for your trouble, 'You can save dollars if you trade at Wanacoopers,'" the author rails. "Something must be done about it," he demands, "government regulation perhaps."[23] *That* never came to pass; instead, radio manufacturers offered the remote control as a solution for frustrated listeners. With a remote control, you would no longer have to subject your families to crass marketeering or cross the room to turn down the radio every time another corporate jingle came on. Finally, it promised, listeners could remain physically passive while vigilantly monitoring for salesmen and hucksters.

Tapping into consumers' desires for control over commercial media proved the key to the remote control's long-term success. By the early 1930s, Americans were quite concerned about the corrupting power of radio advertisements, especially where women and children were concerned. Many editorialists and social commentators worried that women were being brainwashed by the sponsors of daytime radio melodramas. In 1930, WGN in Chicago started broadcasting serial narratives aimed specifically at female homemakers. These programs were called soap operas because the first of them, *Clara, Lu, and Em* (1930–7, 1942–5), was sponsored by Colgate-Palmolive. Critics railed against the soap operas' gossipy content and explicit commercialism, but the soap opera was just the first genre to offer "entertainment wrapped in commercial messages."[24] By 1936, US radio was "an almost purely commercial medium," and listeners complained about the incessant hawking of consumer goods.[25] Radio receivers were now conduits that brought the public world of the marketplace into the private world of the home. As a result, gender-specific anxieties about soap operas gave way to broader misgivings about the effects of radio advertising on family life. Radio drew the family together for entertainment, but its commercials also transformed them into a collection of potential consumers. Many social commentators viewed this transformation with alarm, claiming it turned "a valuable social resource into an instrument of torture."[26] Remote controls were supposed to solve this problem by helping listeners avoid advertisements—that is, helping them listen to more radio!

But instead of quieting advertisements, remote controls often performed precisely the opposite function: they made radios louder. Although the cords on radio remote controls were not very long (twenty feet on average), they encouraged listeners to sit further from their radios and potentially play them at higher volumes than they had before. In February 1930, radio journalist J. D. Relyea observed that remote controls produced problems "in regard to the volume control … due to the fact that the long lead carrying the power [to the remote] must be run through the house."[27] Relyea describes the issue rather obliquely, but it's a problem we've all faced. Remote controls allow you to sit further from your stereo or television set, but sitting further away requires that you turn up the volume. So although these devices were being sold to help listeners shush theirs radios, they were also contributing to the problem they were supposed to solve.

Throughout the 1920s and 1930s, most manufacturers and industry experts continued to imagine remote controls as wired accessories for living room receivers. Yet some science writers and amateur tinkerers tried to re-envision remote control as a radical experiment in home and radio design, even as a merger between the two. Remote controls didn't have to be limited to console attachments; perhaps the entire concept of the console could be eradicated! In a 1930 article for *Popular Science Monthly*, Alfred P. Lane predicted that, "if the idea of remote control captures the popular fancy, future radio receivers will no longer be housed in fine cabinets. They will lose their status as parlour ornaments."[28] Lane proposed that the radio receiver move into a metal box in an attic or basement while loudspeakers and remote control panels be embedded directly in the walls like electrical sockets. In effect, the house itself would become a giant radio cabinet.

*Popular Science Monthly* accompanied Lane's article with an illustration of a beautiful single-family home, part of its façade cut away to reveal Mother in the living room, Father in his basement workshop, and Daughter at her vanity, all connected by radio (see figure 6). With each person engaged in solitary pursuits, the wires connecting their remote controls seem to be the only connection this family shares. Lane's remote control doesn't bring the family together physically, as radio does in most 1930 advertisements. Instead it provides isolated listeners with a common soundtrack, a kind of remote intimacy. Lane's article envisions a new family

**FIGURE 6** Home-as-radio: An illustration from Alfred P. Lane's "Radio Aims at Remote Control," *Popular Science Monthly* (November 1930).

dynamic. Forget the living room and its dream of communal recreation. With remote control, Lane hypothesized, families might enjoy entertainment and privacy at once.

If Lane's prediction sounds ridiculous, remember that many homes are now equipped with multi-room entertainment systems (either wired or wireless) that allow families to play music all over the house from a remote location. In the twenty-first century, we regard multi-room or "multi-zone" home audio systems as speaker set-ups, because advertisers have sold them to us that way. That distinction was not yet in place in 1930, however, so there was no reason for Lane not to consider his arrangement as a form of remote control. Really, it's just a historical accident—the success of one interpretation of "remote control" over another—that makes us limit the term to portable handheld gadgets. Today we don't typically consider a device to be a remote control if we have to get up and cross the room to use it. We want our remotes to be easy to carry anywhere lest we be required to get up. It's rather ironic: we expect remote controls to be mobile because we don't want to be.

The last truly distinctive radio remote, Philco's Mystery Control, was also the first portable radio remote—or maybe I should say *barely portable*, since the Mystery Control was almost nine inches square and over five inches thick. The Mystery Control was the first wireless remote control for radio receivers—"the most thrilling invention since radio itself," according to Philco.[29] Philco started hosting public demonstrations of this thrilling invention in 1938 and claimed that one Philadelphia exhibition caused such a stir that it stopped traffic on the street where it was taking place.[30] The Mystery Control was rather peculiar looking; instead of wires or traditional tuning dials, it featured only a rotary wheel for eight station presets plus volume up and volume down (see figure 7). Rotating the tuning dial would activate a battery-powered oscillator in the device and send a series of low-frequency pulses to a special receiver in the console. Each station on the rotary wheel triggered a different number of pulses from the oscillator, which is how the receiver determined whether to change the station or adjust the volume. Philco allayed consumer anxiety about wireless technology by promising that the Mystery Control did not use a "radio beam," which was technically correct since it used radio waves, not a beam. Philco suggested that Mystery Control users "carry it like a book to any place you wish in your home." The device was effective up to twenty-five feet from its receiver, but this range decreased radically if there was a second Mystery Control remote operating nearby. Also, the device needed to be plugged into an electrical socket to work. The Mystery Control was not really wireless in other words; it just didn't need to be wired into its receiver to work.

Mystery Controls continue to inspire much public curiosity in antiques auctions and online video demonstrations, but they did little to increase remote control consumption during their manufacture period (1939–42). In fact, communications historian Patrick Parsons estimates that no

ENJOY THE THRILL OF THE NEW

# PHILCO
## *Mystery Control*

No wires.. No plug-in.. No cords
of any kind! Yet it runs the
new Philco from any room..
from any place.. in your home!

ONCE MORE, Philco inventive genius makes your daily life easier, happier, more comfortable. Philco engineers have produced a new radio miracle—Philco Mystery Control. *Miraculous, unbelievable* today . . . *household necessity tomorrow* . . . like your telephone, your electric light, like radio itself!

Now, in a new, astonishing way, you are free of the troublesome jumping up and down, the running back and forth to change a program on the radio. Are you reading comfortably in your chair? Are you playing bridge? Are you dining? Are you working in the kitchen, resting on the porch or perhaps reading in bed? *Stay where you are . . . don't move a step . . . don't budge from your chair!* With Philco Mystery Control, wherever you may be in your home, a mere flick of your finger changes stations, regulates volume and even turns off the Mystery Control radio in your living room!

Remember, Philco Mystery Control has *no wires, no plug-in, no cords of any kind.* Carry it around to any place in your home, take it from chair to chair, hand it from one person to another. It has no connection to the radio, house current or anything else. And still, by an unseen, almost magic power, you operate the radio as if you were standing right in front of it!

**See it! Try it! Buy it! Enjoy it!** The Philco dealer near your home is ready to demonstrate and explain the wonders of Philco Mystery Control —without obligation. It's worth your while to visit him . . . *today!* The *easiest* of Monthly Terms make Philco Mystery Control truly easy to buy. Liberal Trade-in Allowance! Ask your Philco dealer.

**PHILCO MYSTERY CONTROL** *consists of the radio and a separate Mystery Control unit.*

Since the control unit has no wire connections of any kind to the radio or anything else, you can carry it easily, in one hand, and place it wherever you may wish in your home. At any chair in the living room, in the dining room, kitchen or bedroom, upstairs or downstairs, even outside on your porch or lawn. And then, by simply turning the dial, you operate the radio in your living room —change stations, control volume, turn the radio off!

**FIGURE 7** "A new radio miracle": A 1938 advertisement for the Philco Mystery Control.

more than 4 percent of electric radios produced during the 1930s had remote controls.[31] Most Americans encountered remote control as a concept in a magazine or store display; it was a curiosity or fantasy during these years rather than a common household device. Still, radio remotes established and stabilized the concept of the media remote control. They determined its general function and shape for future electronic devices, including television. After the Second World War, television replaced radio as the dominant cultural medium, and most electronics manufacturers stopped producing radio remotes in order to concentrate on television instead. Television was a more physically inhibiting medium than radio—since viewers need to be able to see their receivers as well as hear them—but portability nevertheless became an even more important feature for television remotes than it had been for radio. So although most radio remotes were large, full-function boxes, early television remotes often limited themselves to a single button in order to fit comfortably in the palm of your hand.

*     *     *

The first television remote was the Telezoom, introduced by Garod in 1948.[32] The Telezoom had one button that, when clicked, caused the television to zoom in on the image in the center of the frame. It was small, approximately an inch thick and two inches in diameter, so you could hold it easily in your hand while clicking the button with your thumb. Early television screens were also small, small enough that a zoom function might have been useful for some viewers, but television was also novel and exciting. Perhaps that's why there was never much demand for the Telezoom remote.

In any event, the first *successful* television remote was the equally petite Lazy Bones, created by Zenith and introduced to the home market in 1950. No one at Zenith remembers who originally invented the Lazy Bones, but its technology strongly resembled one of Zenith's radio remotes—if anything, it was less complicated than its predecessors.[33] Like a radio receiver remote, the Lazy Bones was connected to its console by a seventeen-foot cable. That cord was thinner, more flexible, and easier to move, however. It was not designed to be fixed to the floor but functioned like a tether for its little bullet-shaped remote. The Lazy Bones only had two buttons—one black, the other white—that adjusted the tuner clockwise or counterclockwise by a single station. It added $30 to the price of any Zenith television set at a time when sets ranged in price between $269 and $629. It could also be purchased separately and installed by a handy homeowner or television repairman. $30 in 1950 is equivalent to nearly $300 today, though, so the Lazy Bones remote still represented an extravagant expense for middle-class consumers.

Zenith's Lazy Bones was an explicit response to commercial advertising in broadcast television. Television broadcasting began in 1939, but the Second World War and the demands of wartime manufacturing stalled the industry through the mid-1940s. It was not until 1947 that television became a stable, commercially viable medium. Many early television networks got their start in radio, so it should come as no surprise that they too relied on advertisers to sponsor programs. Like radio stations, television stations made money by assembling audiences for advertisers, and like radio audiences, television audiences resented commercial interruptions. Then as now, audiences interpreted television as entertainment medium rather than an advertising platform and were appalled by the crass endorsements pouring from their new devices.

Zenith's founder and president, Eugene F. McDonald Jr, was particularly averse to television commercials and used his company to fight them. He believed that if television manufacturers made it easier for audiences to tune away from or mute commercials, advertisers and broadcasters would have to improve their pitches or find a new business model altogether. Hence Zenith was also testing the first pay-per-view television system in the early 1950s, which it called Phonevision. Phonevision would enable viewers to watch Hollywood movies for one dollar each via a set-top descrambler connected to the television's antenna and a telephone line. Phonevision never got beyond localized testing, but the Lazy Bones did, and proved quite effective at helping viewers change the station on irritating commercials. Thus the Lazy Bones remote control was Zenith's most influential contribution to a mostly forgotten mid-century debate about the best business model for broadcast television.

Zenith emphasized its war on television commercials in many of its Lazy Bones advertisements. One early advertisement for the Lazy Bones depicts a man sitting in his easy chair, legs crossed, smiling at the image of a young boy singing on his television set. The gentleman seems to be enjoying his show, but he nevertheless holds a Lazy Bones remote aloft in his right hand, thumb over the black button, as if waiting for that inevitable commercial interruption. In between the man and his television is a picture of Zenith's "Turret Tuner," the "miracle of automatic precision and stability" that makes push-button remote control possible.[34] The Turret Tuner figuratively takes the place of the Lazy Bones's cord, which is nowhere to be seen. It's a visual sleight of hand that gives the viewer the impression that the Turret Tuner is part of the remote control. This allows the Lazy Bones ad to emphasize the remote control's power instead of its limitations. The name "Turret Tuner" also associates remote control with wartime virility, perhaps as compensation for the Lazy Bones's rather emasculating epithet. It crucially changes the reader's perception of the Lazy Bones and its user, the man in the advertisement. He isn't just idly watching a young boy sing on TV. No, he's on alert, an active participant in the television apparatus. This serviceman still has his finger on the trigger, ready to tune to a new station anytime his television fails to please him.

Other 1951 ads for the Lazy Bones feature family audiences rather than a solitary male viewer, but in each the man is always the one in control of the remote. There's one particularly prevalent image from of Zenith's Lazy Bones campaign that depicts a father, mother and son sitting in matching armchairs before a majestic television console (see figure 8). Mother holds Junior while Father holds the remote control. Above them a legend reads, "It's like something out of Arabian Nights! From across the room— without ever leaving your easy chair—you change television programs with a small, streamlined control that fits cozily in the palm of your hand!"[35] *You* here is clearly Father, the one in possession of the remote control. He's the largest figure in the illustration and the subject of its copy, the king of his castle and the wonderful world of television. The ad implies that men should be in command of the television and hints that women cannot be trusted with that responsibility. In other words, Zenith employs the logic of patriarchy to encourage

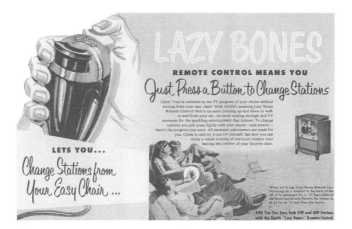

FIGURE 8 "Try it for yourself": An illustration from a 1951 flier for Zenith's Lazy Bones remote control.

male consumers to buy remotes and exert control over the newest member of his household, his television.

Another image within this same ad shows a manicured female hand holding the Lazy Bones device, however. This detail might seem incongruous given the patriarchal dynamics in the ad's main illustration and copy, but it is important to note that this hand appears entirely on its own. It is not attached to a body, let alone a family scene. The female hand *models* the Lazy Bones, then, rather than using it. This distinction is important, because it means that this image continues the gendered logic of the rest of the ad. The female hand makes the Lazy Bones seem more attractive and desirable, while subtle sexist suppositions about women's technical abilities hint that it is must also be easy to use. So even though a female hand does hold a remote in Zenith's advertisement, the ad still suggests that remote controls are for men. Women may use remote controls, but they are present in this ad to reinforce the power that remotes offer male users, not to wield that power themselves.

Junior's role in the illustration also conveys an important fantasy about how remote controls might improve family dynamics. The boy sits in his mother's lap while his comic books lie abandoned on the floor. Something has possessed him to discard his comics in favor of a boring piano performance on TV. Is he transported by a sudden affection for classical music? Doubtful. It seems more likely that the boy has been drawn in by his father's masterful use of an exciting new technology. The ad suggests that remote control can help fulfill cultural fantasies about television as an "electric hearth." As television historian Lynn Spigel has demonstrated, mid-century television manufacturers and broadcasters tried to reassure TV-wary households that television could enhance family life. Relatives would gather around the set the way earlier generations of Americans gathered around the fire. Spigel finds that postwar television programs and advertisements contributed to a new ideology of suburban domesticity for the bedroom communities springing up around the United States in the wake of the Second World War and the Eisenhower Interstate Act.[36] Television played a vital role in teaching audiences what it meant to be suburban and how to adapt traditional family values to this new scene. This Lazy Bones ad reveals that remote control was very much a part of that cultural agenda and 1950s fantasies of the "good life." Remote controls would be the scepters for all the lords of the manor that this new model of private home ownership was generating.[37] Unfortunately, there are no industry statistics on how many Lazy Bones remotes Zenith sold or whether people used these devices to realize the kinds of domestic idylls such ads depicted. Circumstantial evidence suggests that in fact the Lazy Bones was not widely adopted, since few cities in the United States in 1950 received more than one or two television channels, and the Lazy Bones's sole function was to switch between stations.

Still, the Lazy Bones did provide a precedent for remote control within the television industry and television culture more broadly. Within a few years, the Lazy Bones had a fleet of imitators, including RCA's Magic Brain remote (a spin-off of their patented Magic Brain tuners), the Conrac Fleetwood, the Silvertone Medalist and others from Emerson, General Electric, Packard-Bell, Philco, Sentinal and Tech Master. Many of these devices were aftermarket accessories that a television owner could attach to an existing set. Their powers were limited but diverse. They ranged from merely turning the TV on and off or advancing the tuner by one station at a time to fully variable volume control, image adjustment and brightness control. These early television remotes also took a variety of shapes, from a push-button bullet at the end of a long chord (e.g., Zenith and Philco) to a large metal box covered in dials and switches and featuring an auxiliary loudspeaker (e.g., Packard-Bell).

Major manufacturers were not the only ones imagining how television remotes could benefit suburban families. Independent entrepreneurs like Howard Manischewitz (yes, *that* Manischewitz) created and sold aftermarket remotes that could perform the same function as manufacturers' but at a fraction of the price. Of all the mid-century independent remotes, Manischewitz's Blab-Off was the most famous, perhaps because it was also the first. His daughter recalls that the idea for remote control came to him in late 1952, while watching television with her mother:

> "There ought to be a way to shut off the blab without running over to the TV," my mother griped. "It'll wake the kids."

"Easy," said my father. "I could invent a way in ten minutes, it's that simple."

...

While my mother timed him, my father ran to the basement and returned with twenty feet of lamp cord, a scissors, a Gilbert on-off line switch, electrical tape, and a flashlight. He got back on the floor by the TV console, put it together, and presto, it worked.[38]

The Blab-Off made its commercial debut in March 1953. Sales took off after Walter Winchell mentioned the device on his ABC television show, allegedly referring to it as "the most terrifying gadget in television for TV set owners."[39] Alpern must be misremembering Winchell's comment, or maybe Winchell was projecting, because the Blab-Off was actually quite popular with television set owners. By November 1953, Manischewitz had sold 15,000 remotes, and a *Reader's Digest* survey revealed that 95 percent of Blab-Off users were "completely or very well-satisfied" with their remotes. *Reader's Digest* hailed the Blab-Off as "simplicity itself," commending its powers and assuring readers that "the device is absolutely safe." So confident was Manischewitz in his invention that he sold it with a "satisfaction-or-money-back guarantee" and openly boasted that his success might put him out of business. "If the day should come," he told *Reader's Digest*, "when most TV sets have this cutter-outer, Blab-Off will then probably have accomplished its mission."

Like Eugene F. McDonald, Manischewitz dreamed that "a few million people equipped with this freedom of selection ought eventually to raise the caliber of TV commercials to the point where *Blab-Off* will no longer be necessary."[40]

Manischewitz intended the Blab-Off to rescue "the helpless TV audience" from irritating commercials, and from the story of its invention to the grateful notes from readers, that audience is routinely figured as a family.[41] Remote control would allegedly be the family's greatest tool and its manufacturer their greatest friend as they battled advertisers for control over their private sphere. This conflict characterized the marketing of the first generation of wireless remote controls too, beginning with Zenith's futuristic Flash-Matic and its ultrasonic "clicker," the Space Command. Unlike the Lazy Bones, these remotes featured a mute button explicitly designed for quieting noisy advertisements. In fact, *mute* was the first remote control function not explicitly available on the console itself (the Telezoom's poor, unpopular zoom command not withstanding).

As wireless remotes became more popular, the devices would gradually transition from accessories to proper features of television design. They became a major component of the television culture reshaping domestic routines across the United States. Like their wired predecessors, wireless remote controls changed home design and family dynamics while also encouraging a new mode of television consumption, namely channel surfing. It would require the cable station proliferation of the 1980s for channel surfing to really come into its own, but even in the 1960s remote controls facilitated more profligate television consumption. As the next chapter will demonstrate, after 1955 remote controls were no longer just gadgets. They would continue changing volumes and values, channels and culture, more and more with each passing decade.

# 2. CONVENIENCE, NECESSITY, NUISANCE

Think back to 1991, to the days before electronic program guides (EPGs), those interactive media menus that became ubiquitous in the late 1990s. Remember what it felt like to sit on the couch, remote control in hand, clicking through as fast as you could to discover what was on all of the thirty-three channels your cable service provided.[1] That was channel surfing. It was a historically specific response to a particular intersection of technologies: infrared remote controls, satellite cable delivery, and a widening array of niche television channels.

The term *channel surfing* is a peculiar metaphor for this method of remote control television viewing. It first appeared in print in a 1986 *Wall Street Journal* article on televised election coverage.[2] Channel surfers alarmed more staid viewers by surveying simultaneous broadcasts swiftly, superficially—some might even say hyperactively. Their detractors tended to dismiss channel surfers as lazy and dimwitted, but channel surfing was a totally reasonable and intuitive response to its particular moment in television history. Much as surfers float suspended on the surface of the water in an intuitive engagement with the waves and tides, channel surfers skimmed over dozens of television channels. Using their remote controls, they coasted between stations, never getting bogged down in one program until they'd considered every option. While channel surfers may not have had a deep appreciation of the shows they rushed past, they understood the ethos of the remote control: sit back, relax, and go with the flow of your ever-expanding entertainment options.

Between 1955 and 1985, wireless remote controls helped create a new television culture in the United States. Television culture emerges when we allow our lives to be ruled by the box, when broadcast schedules and television technologies orchestrate our domestic routines and shape our popular culture. During the mid-twentieth century, television culture inspired new gender norms, social routines—even home furnishings. And though remote controls would not make it into a majority of US households until 1986, they were part of a network of objects, corporations, and people leading that great social change. Remotes represented an important aspirational norm of television culture. By *aspirational norm* I mean a cultural ideal that many share even if few participate in it directly. Private home ownership is an aspirational norm; so is the 24-inch waist. During the mid-twentieth century, wireless remote control became an aspirational norm and influenced what people thought television could or should be, even if they did not own the devices themselves.[3] Wireless remotes made television, as we now know it, possible.

Consider the twenty-first-century widescreen HDTV. Why would anyone want a television set so large that she has to sit across the room from it, unless it comes with a remote control? Now consider how domestic architecture and interior decoration have changed alongside these massive sets. Over the past thirty years, open-concept living areas have become a dominant trend in US home design. Widescreen television sets work well in open-concept living rooms where couches and easy chairs are typically over twenty feet from the set itself. Remote controls make television viewing practical for open-concept houses. They are a small but crucial part of how we live with TV and a telling example of how the ways that living with TV has changed our daily lives.

Wireless remote controls obviously improved on the cumbersome technology of wired remote controls, but they retained the basic social fantasies attached to those devices. As I discuss in Chapter 1, radio remotes were marketed first as luxuries and later as tools to silence irritating commercials. Advertisers used the same rhetoric for television remotes, trumpeting both wired and wireless remotes' ability to keep the family safe from the corrupting influence of marketers. Through it all, the armchair remained a prominent component of remote control rhetoric: get a remote, and you'll never have to get out of your easy chair again. Technology does not have to be disruptive or even discomfiting, the advertisers promised, as long as you purchase this additional technological device to manage it.

But while radio remotes were designed to provide stationary, secondary tuning stations (due to their bothersome cords), television remote controls were mobile—even if most users chose to employ them from the comfort of that oft-mentioned easy chair. Beginning in the mid-1950s advertisers exploited the portability of wireless remote controls, rebranding "control" as "freedom"—what Sony would one day call "the freedom of total control." In fact the terms *freedom* and *power* became almost interchangeable in late twentieth-century ads for consumer electronics. They helped convince us that remote control was the same thing as active engagement with the media. Remotes do offer many conveniences, but the "freedom" to sit back passively and choose is not the same thing as cultural intervention.

By 1985 aspirational norm of remote control had become normal, and it was failing to live up to the fantasy. During the early 1980s, infrared technology made remote controls cheaper and more common. At first, inexpensive remote control seemed like a dream come true, but as more and more manufacturers added remote controls to their devices, convenience turned into a nuisance. Today, the majority of US households have four or more remote controls strewn about their living room, and power over remote controls is now its own issue.[3]

But we're getting ahead of ourselves. In order to understand where channel surfing and remote control clutter came from, we need to return to 1955 when Zenith introduced the first wireless television remote control as nothing short of a space-age marvel. Several cultural forces would influence the wireless remote control between 1955 and 1985, including changing gender roles, the rise of cable broadcasting, and the emergence of home video. As I argue in Chapter 1, remote control is a media-manufactured solution to media-produced problems. So it should come as no surprise that when the problem of remote control clutter began bothering viewers in the mid-1980s, the solution turned out to be *another* remote control. Maybe remotes are tools after all, but if so, then they're tools for the promotion of television, not control over it.

*    *    *

The first television set controlled by wireless remote was the Zenith's Flash-Matic, which came with a "flash tuner" remote control that looked delightfully ahead of its time (see figure 9). The flash tuner—or "flash gun" as ads deemed it—resembled a ray gun from a science fiction movie.[4] The flash gun was a major departure from the traditionalist aesthetic dominating television console design. In fact that aesthetic even included the Flash-Matic set, which was almost as conventional in appearance as the flash gun was outlandish. As had been the case for phonograph and radio, most television designers sought to integrate TV consoles into established furniture styles. Of course there were some exciting art deco exceptions to this rule, but

**FIGURE 9** A 1955 Zenith Flash-Matic "flash gun" remote control. Photo used by permission of Steve Pearlman.

most manufacturers eschewed modernist designs. They didn't want to emphasize the machine as machine. When the prevailing wisdom was that women wanted their electronics to blend in with other home décor. As a result, most 1920s, 1930s, and 1940s remote controls were designed to be inconspicuous—anything but flashy. Zenith's flash gun overturned such staid principles to embrace the Space Age then capturing the American imagination. Capitalizing on a mid-century popular fascination with science, engineering, and aeronautics, Zenith designed the flash gun to make television viewing feel like part of a high-tech future. Its ads even depicted the flash gun's "flash of magic light" as a laser beam shooting from the gun to the television set (see figure 10). The laser wouldn't be invented until 1958, so Zenith's flash gun really did seem to be a device of the future, and a violent one at that.

Zenith marketed this violent new futuristic remote as a device to empower a singular viewer. This was a major departure from previous remote control ad campaigns (discussed in Chapter 1), which emphasized family togetherness. The Flash-Matic's ads abandoned such traditionalism to capitalize on Space Age individualism. Zenith promised that the Flash-Matic's flash gun would let you "shoot off annoying commercials from across the room" with "a flash of magic light."[5] Addressing a singular "you," the Flash-Matic ad made its remote control sharp-shooter sound like a hero rather than a passive consumer. This gunman would be an active, discerning viewer, not just another slack-jawed subject of mass-media propaganda. Media brainwashing was a particular fear of the era. Following the Second World War, sociologists and public intellectuals warned the public against the "narcotizing" effects of mass media, the ways it promoted entertainment over intellectual or political engagement.[6] The flash gun's pistol-like appearance and the combative rhetoric Zenith used to market it promised to make complacent viewers active again.

That transformation was particularly important for male viewers, who were allegedly being emasculated by the feminizing passivity of television viewing.[7] But male models were never used in Flash-Matic advertisements. In the

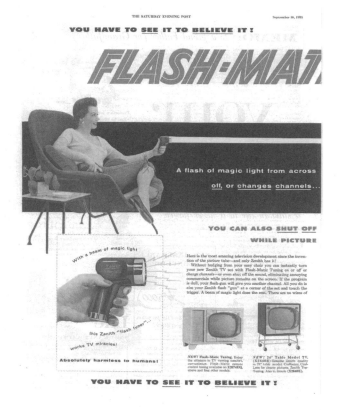

**FIGURE 10** "A flash of magic light": A 1955 advertisement for the Zenith Flash-Matic television set with "flash gun".

**IC TUNING** BY ZENITH

## ONLY ZENITH HAS IT !

the room (no wires, no cords) turns set **on**,

and you remain in your easy chair

**LONG, ANNOYING COMMERCIALS**

**REMAINS ON SCREEN**

*The Bismarck.* (Model X2261EQ), 21". Flash-Matic Tuning. New Royal "X" Chassis. 10" speaker. CinéBeam, Ciné-Lens, Spotlite Dial. Hand-grained finish cabinet on casters. Also in mahogany color (X2261EQ). As low as $395.95.*

any kind to trip you or tangle you. No mechanisms or contraptions to clutter up your living room. This is not an accessory. This is a built-in, integral part of *several* new Zenith Royalty TV receivers.

Let your Zenith dealer show you the famous Zenith features such as CinéBeam,* Ciné-Lens, Top Tuning, 20,000 Volts of Picture Power, and this latest achievement in creative electronics—Flash-Matic Tuning. It makes your television set a home theater! But you have to see it to believe it. Stop at your Zenith dealer's soon.

**Also see the other outstanding new Zenith models just announced**

*IF IT'S NEW, IT'S FROM ZENITH!*

# ZENITH

**The Royalty of TELEVISION and radio**

Backed by 36 years of leadership in radionics exclusively

ALSO MAKERS OF FINE HEARING AIDS

Zenith Radio Corporation, Chicago 39, Illinois

*Manufacturer's suggested retail price. Slightly higher in Far West and South.

*NEW! Over-and-Under 21" TV-Phonograph.* (X2298E). In one handsome cabinet, superb picture quality; exclusive Cobra-Matic* record player. Also in mahogany color (X2298E).

*NEW! Jet Tuning Table Models.* The set that brings television to every room in the house! Compact, conventional, colorful. Two-tone color combinations. (X2223Y, shown.)

Flash-Matic's most ubiquitous ad, a buxom young woman in a low-cut yellow sweater and pedal pushers smiles as she lifts her flash gun toward the television set. Her outfit, pose, and make-up sexualize her; like the flash gun, this model is designed for visual appeal. Curled up in her modernist armchair next to a nice houseplant, she reassures the viewer that the flash gun is not intimidating or dangerous—just hip. She even shoots from the hip, a casual yet confident pose that emphasizes her sexuality. Female models were integral to the Flash-Matic's marketing campaign. Without exception, Flash-Matic advertisements typically pictured a woman pulling the trigger. These female models balanced the violent connotations of the flash gun's design and the advertisement's copy, and they also naturalized the device, making it seem more attractive and approachable. Only the cover of the Flash-Matic user's manual depicts a man holding a flash gun. Of course, that picture was intended for customers who had already purchased a Flash-Matic television set, so it served a different purpose than the marketing campaign. A manual doesn't need to convince potential buyers. Instead it addresses new users directly. That's why the Flash-Matic manual can depict a man in a suit firing his flash gun at a smiling female television star. Its purpose is to excite the consumer and affirm his decision to purchase a Flash-Matic. It reassures him that the flash gun will enhance his active control over the media and, by extension, his virility. If only the damned things had worked!

In theory, users could control their Flash-Matic television sets by shooting beams of light from the flash gun at photosensitive cells in the four corners of the Flash-Matic television screen. Each cell had a different function: to mute the sound, adjust the channel up or down, and turn the set on or off. The Flash-Matic's phototechnology represented a radical innovation in wireless signal transfer, which was previously limited to radio. But because the Flash-Matic's photosensors responded to full-spectrum light, they could be activated by any light source, including a light bulb or the sun. Any beam of light coming from the correct angle could turn the set on or off, and all too often it did. Owners of Flash-Matic television sets therefore had to position the consoles carefully in relation to windows and mirrors and potentially relocate their lamps as well. After all, the Flash-Matic's flash gun was really just a fancy-looking flashlight. It was easy to replace, but its medium—light—was also too common to be a practical communications medium.

It gets worse. Because the Flash-Matic's photosensitive cells worked on contrast, the living room needed to be comparatively dark for the flash gun signal to register. Dimming the lights makes it difficult for people in the room to do anything besides watch television. That was a major setback in an era when families still idealized television as an electric hearth. Flash-Matics also malfunctioned when the flash gun's batteries grew weak and when the remote was more than twenty feet away from the console. Natural light diffusion also often led to the wrong photocells picking up a flash gun flash. Flash-Matics were glitchy, but they weren't cheap, retailing for around $395 in 1955 ($3,443 today). That's $250 more than the cheapest Zenith sets.[8] So it should come as no surprise that Zenith only sold 30,000 Flash-Matics during their one year on the market, a year in which over 5.7 million television sets were produced in the United States alone.[9] Sadly, the Flash-Matic proved just a flash in the pan.

Instead of abandoning wireless remote control technology, Zenith replaced the Flash-Matic flash gun with the first ultrasonic remote control, the Space Command 200 (see figure 11). Unlike their predecessors, ultrasonic remotes were both wireless and reliable—and silent, except for a slight click when the small push-button hammers inside the remote struck their ultrasonic tuning rods. As *Electronics World* explained in 1960, the Space Command's "resonant bars or rods … function in the manner of tuning forks," producing tones too high in frequency for humans to hear (approximately 40.0 kilohertz).[10] A special microphone receiver hidden in the television set would detect these ultrasonic signals and process them as commands.

Truthfully, the Space Command could not do much, but what it could do was revolutionary. The first Space Command, the 200, had two tuning rods and two functions: mute and channel up. The Space Command 400, added two more tuning rods and two more commands—power on/off and channel down—but Zenith had reached the limit of tuning rods it could include. Subsequent Space Command models would use combinations of tones to offer additional

The one and only thing NEW in television!

# ZENITH
# "SPACE-COMMAND" TV TUNER

It answers silent commands from your easy chair...or even from the next room. Turns set on and off, changes stations, mutes sound, shuts off long annoying commercials!

You'll be amazed! There's nothing between you and the television set but space! No wires, no cords, no batteries, no radio control waves! Yet the "SPACE-COMMANDER" control box in your hand carries out your commands from across the room, or even from the next room. Is it magic? How does it work? Well, *see* it yourself... *try* it yourself at your Zenith dealer's. You've just never seen anything like it! And remember—only Zenith has it!

NOTHING BETWEEN YOU AND THE SET BUT SPACE

You hear nothing!

You see nothing!

No batteries!

No cords! No wires!

No flashlights!

No radio control waves!

No transistors!

The only wireless complete remote control!

**ZENITH**
®

The Royalty of RADIO,
TELEVISION and PHONOGRAPHS
Backed by 37 years of leadership in radionics exclusively
ALSO MAKERS OF FINE HEARING AIDS • Zenith Radio Corporation, Chicago 39, Ill.

*189*

**FIGURE 11** "The one and only NEW thing in television": A 1956 advertisement for Zenith's Space Command 200 remote control.

commands, but not many. The finite number of possible tonal combinations limited the Space Command's functionality.

All the same, the Space Command was a milestone in remote control development, since it did not need to be connected to its receiver and was far more dependable than the Flash-Matic. It also did not require batteries, which was a major selling point in an age when battery-operated electronics were unusual, even off-putting to many consumers. Because the Space Command's high frequency tones did not travel well from room to room, moreover, you could own and operate multiple Space Commands within one house without interference. Finally, Zenith had created the first fully functional wireless remote control. The Space Command established the precedents for remote control design, use, and marketing that manufacturers would follow for decades to come.

In fact, some manufacturers followed Zenith's model a little too closely. In February 1958, Zenith sued the Admiral Corporation for multiple counts of patent infringement, including suspicious similarities between its Space Command and Admiral's own ultrasonic remotes. Admiral had been selling a remote control device known as Son-R since 1956 to manage its high-end multi-component entertainment centers (see figure 12).[11] Initially Admiral borrowed some engineering principles from the Space Command to make its Son-R remote, but when the Son-R proved faulty, Admiral decided to borrow more than just principles. In the words of US District Court Judge Ross Rizley, "Admiral engineers

**FIGURE 12** "Tiny as milady's compact": A 1961 advertisement for Admiral's Son-R remote control.

decided to go straight down the pathway Zenith had tracked out. In fact, they even went so far as to hire a former Zenith engineer to reveal trade secrets."[12] Rizley decided the suit in Zenith's favor and ordered a permanent injunction against Admiral to stop further production of p remotes.[13]

Zenith also saw competition from Motorola, RCA, Westinghouse, Hoffman, and other companies selling wireless ultrasonic and low-powered radio-frequency remotes during the 1950s and 1960s. Some came with a television set while others were aftermarket accessories (like the Blab-Off discussed in Chapter 1), but all were far less popular than the Space Command. Radio-frequency remotes were less reliable than ultrasonics because they might share frequencies with a neighbor's set, which led to crosstalk. They were also subject to atmospheric and electrical interference that never bothered ultrasonic remotes. Not that ultrasonics were problem-free; all of the first-generation ultrasonic controls (those that used one tone per command) could be activated by high frequency noise like loose change jingling or door hinges squeaking. Many manufacturers resolved this problem by modifying their remote control systems to operate according to a two-tone method, but other issues proved more difficult to fix. These included reliable tuning and consistent image control. As *Consumer Reports* noted in 1959,

> There are a number of attributes which are highly desirable in any TV set, and quite essential in a remote-controlled set. These include good automatic gain control, or AGC

(automatic compensation for variations in signal strength from channel to channel), good synchronization (which holds the picture in place horizontally and vertically), and a good stable tuner, which, once it has been adjusted to bring in the best possible picture on each channel, needs readjustment only occasionally.[14]

*Consumer Reports* was trying to suggest that users' physical passivity and comfort—their desire not to get up and fiddle with dials or antennas—were the basis of remote control, the key to its appeal. Without a high-end set capable of stable tuning, steady image hold, and powerful AGC, that passivity would be ruined. A person might pay a lot for remote control only to have to get up again and again to adjust the picture or fine-tune the reception. *Buyers beware*, the article warned: many mid-century televisions could be wired for remote control, but not all were up to the challenge.

Despite these difficulties and despite their expense, remote controls were an aspirational norm of television culture during the 1950s. During those years, remote controls were sold with roughly 10 percent of color television sets and 1 percent of black and white television sets. Black and white set sales far exceeded those of color sets, though, so only a tiny fraction of new television sets sold in the postwar period came with remote controls. The device also added as much as $40 to $100 to the cost of a new television set ($327 to $818 today), so few consumers actually purchased them. Still, ads for remote controls appeared regularly in popular periodicals such as

*The Saturday Evening Post* and *Ladies' Home Journal*, not to mention science and technology magazines. Together with fictional stories and television shows about remote controls, they guaranteed public awareness of the technology.[15]

Advertisements for remote controls also contributed to television culture's influence on US gender norms. As television allegedly feminized male viewers, remote control could allegedly restore their lost masculinity. Consider a 1956 ad for Zenith's Space Command, the first to market remote controls directly to men without the intercession of a female model. In 1956, Zenith heralded the Space Command 400 as "the one and only thing NEW in television" next to a picture of a male hand holding up this miraculous invention. "You hear nothing! You see nothing! No batteries! No cords! No wires! No flashlights!"—and no families or female models.[16] The rest of the ad's rhetoric was pretty conventional, including all the standard promises about how the device "shuts off long annoying commercials" and issues "silent commands from your easy chair." What's really new about the Space Command, then, isn't its rhetoric or its technology, which the ad neither names nor explains. Rather it's the technology's intended beneficiary. Through the absence of women and families in its illustration, Zenith presents the Space Command as a device a man might buy for himself, to improve his own leisure time.

In fact, mid-century male-centered advertising was indicative of a major shift in American gender roles, as Lisa Parks, Max Dawson, and other television historians have shown.[17] Before the 1950s, American masculinity was largely associated with the virtues of "probity, restraint, and thrift."[18] Such qualities were incompatible with 1950s consumer culture, as was the lingering association of shopping with women and women's work. If real men weren't supposed to be interested in conspicuous consumption, how could they participate in the new material economy? Advertisers resolved this issue with images of American men enjoying a little well-earned luxury. After all, didn't the family breadwinner deserve a little convenience when he got home? By identifying such indulgences as high tech, advertisers could also mitigate consumerism's feminine taint. Technology was traditionally marked as masculine after all, so indulging in the latest gadget should affirm a man's virility rather than impugning it. Hence 1950s television manufacturers also encouraged men to build their manliness through home electronics repair. As Lisa Parks explains, a rash of mid-century ads and articles suggested that the inner workings of the television set were too complicated for women but should not intimidate the modern man. Television repair skills could even be a source of pride for men who cultivated them.[19] Many urban areas offered "opportunities for *men* to learn more about television's operation" and thus to enjoy consumer electronics in a masculine context.[20]

Mid-century advertisers also tried to make television and remote controls seem more masculine by associating them with traditional macho icons, such as the cowboy. Cowboys feature prominently in a 1960 ad for the Space Command

400 that depicts a white-collar remote control user getting the upper hand on these manly men (see figure 13). In the ad's illustration, three cowboys lean along a rail fence, one of whom stares off-screen menacingly at someone or something. A male hand in the foreground holds a Space Command 400 aloft. This pose suggests that the anonymous white-collar professional is more powerful and more masculine than them. Those virile cowboys would scoff at the leisure and luxury of remote control, but note that the ad marks them as fictional, as mere entertainment for the man in the white shirt. He does not participate in that kind of physical, working-class brawn; instead he buys remote control over other people and objects. He is both figuratively and metaphorically changing the channel on traditional masculinity, from physical brawn to economic power.

Lastly, note the absence of women and children from this scene. It suggests that remote control can be practiced not just by men but also *for* men. In contrast to the early remote control ads described in Chapter 1—wherein a father wields the remote control for his wife or family—the man holding this Space Command isn't aiming to please anyone but himself. He isn't trying to impress his wife or protect his family from commercial harassment. This Space Command ad invites men to buy and use remote controls for their own satisfaction. That was cutting-edge concept for mid-century American advertising, but it would become even more common in the decades to come.

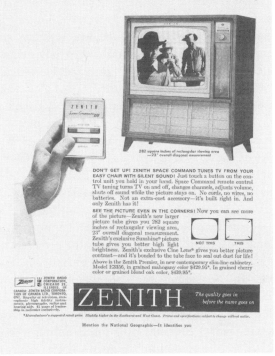

**FIGURE 13** "It's built right in": A 1960 advertisement for Zenith's Space Command 400 remote control.

Zenith also used key celebrity endorsements to counter any assertions that television emasculated men. In a 1957 ad for the Space Command 400, the stars of the popular television sitcom *The George Burns and Gracie Allen Show* sell remote control as spousal control. On the show, Gracie Allen played a "Dumb Dora" housewife whose inane and illogical banter baffled her husband, long-suffering straight man George Burns. On the show, Allen's antics determine plotlines and dominate every conversation, which both amuses and irritates Burns. In their Space Command ad, Burns brandishes a remote control over his shoulder at Allen's image on TV (see figure 14). "Look out, Gracie," he warns. "With the Zenith Space Command TV I can change programs from across the room." Space Command gives Burns the power to tune out his wife's silliness—a power, the ad implies, that many real-world husbands might like as well. "George! You wouldn't dare!" Allen's image protests. Note that Allen doesn't object to Burns's presumption. She too believes he has the power to silence her. She merely questions his nerve, which the reader never doubts. The Burns and Allen ad portrays a far different family dynamic than those depicted in earlier remote control ads. Only seven years prior, the Lazy Bones sold visions of family harmony. Now remote controls were being marketed to men as tools for personal agency to use against their wives. Advertisers felt authorized to exclude or even mock traditional ideals of masculine self-sacrifice and family tranquility.[21]

**FIGURE 14** "Look out, Gracie!": A 1957 advertisement for Zenith's Space Command 400 remote control.

Zenith wasn't the only manufacturer to try celebrity endorsements for remote control. In 1961, RCA hired big band leader Vaughn Monroe to hawk its Wireless Wizard remotes. Monroe's spot cheekily emphasized a new feature of the Wireless Wizard, its ability to turn the television set off completely.[22] Prior to the Wireless Wizard, all wireless remote control systems used separate chasses for their in-set receivers, which meant that the remote control receivers had to be turned on and off separately from the rest of the set. Users couldn't just flop down in a favorite easy chair and start perusing channels. First they had to walk over to the set and turn the remote control receiver on. Monroe's ad was among the first to cast this requirement as an inconvenience, but his pitch should remind us that mid-century television viewers had different expectations for remote control than we do. Remote controls were not designed to eliminate viewers' physical interaction with their television sets but to help them avoid advertisements. They were supposed to make switching between a few channels feel like control over mass media. So to the extent that they encouraged physical passivity, mid-century remotes also encouraged users to equate it with active mental engagement.

*　　*　　*

Remote controls were not the only mid-century devices encouraging television watchers to reorient their homes and lives around TV; other television accessories also conspired to make "settling in" the modus operandi of television viewing. Cultural historian Karal Ann Marling observes that "televiewing entailed movement [or lack thereof] that called wholly new kinds of furniture into being." One key example of this trend is the television tray table, which made its debut in 1952. Folding tables weren't new, but companies like

Cal-Dak now trumpeted them as "perfect for TV dining" in order to cash in on television's growing cultural clout. Rumor had it that President Eisenhower and the First Lady ate dinner in front of their television set, which also sent the popularity of TV tray tables soaring.[23]

As television accessories, TV tray tables and remote controls spoke to television's cultural clout, its power as a way of life rather than just an entertainment medium. They were only two of many consumer goods and appliances adapted or rebranded to support television viewing. There was also Toastmaster's "Television's Twin," a personal-sized portable toaster that came on an individual tray with matching dishes.[24] Toastmaster introduced Television's Twin in 1950 after trying and failing to sell other toaster-themed hospitality sets in the past. No one much wanted to serve guests on toaster-equipped lap trays, but "Television's Twin" reinvented the concept by moving it away from entertaining and toward private convenience. Meanwhile Servel offered a small rolling refrigerator, the Electric Wonderbar, for TV viewers who did not want to get up for a cool drink. Virginia House even sold an entire dinette set on wheels, "wonderful for snacks or even meals while you watch television," that viewers might push out of the way between shows.[25]

But the most famous mid-century television accessory remains the TV dinner. In 1953, Swanson initiated a major advertisement campaign to launch its "TV Brand Dinners." These flash-frozen meals—originally comprised of turkey, stuffing, sweet potatoes, and buttered peas—were sold in paper boxes that looked like wood-grain television consoles. Swanson was not the first company to market premade frozen meals to American consumers, but they were the first to associate prepared food with television. By calling their products "TV Brand Dinners" and advertising them with mottos like "How to catch the early, early show with an easy, easy dinner," Swanson cashed in on mid-century television culture and its upheaval of longstanding social mores. As Marling explains, "The relationship with television further allowed buyers to excuse any change in dining habits represented by the purchase of heat-and-eat cuisine; if it was okay to eat in front of the set, then it was socially acceptable to eat turkey dinners someone else had prepared."[26] That is, eating in front of the TV made it alright to eat prepared foods, and eating prepared foods made it alright to eat in front of the TV. It is a circular logic, but it allowed Swanson to present TV Brand Dinners as both modern conveniences and mere updates of traditional family values.

Swanson's TV Brand Dinners were also designed to capitalize on and reinforce television's reputation as a window on the world. Swanson modeled their three-compartment aluminum serving trays on airplane meal trays, which lent the TV dinners an air of exoticism. Airplane meals at home—what better manifestation could there be of television's promise to take viewers around the world from the comfort of their living rooms? Like remote controls, then, TV dinners gave diners permission to do something passive (i.e., eating prepared foods) by disguising it as something active (i.e., choosing a culinary adventure). Those traditional turkey dinners also helped make TV Brand Dinners feel familiar as well as new; it was a powerful combination. By 1955, Swanson had sold over twenty-five million TV Brand Dinners. Naturally, a number of other food manufacturers tried offering TV-themed meals and snacks, but none were as successful as Swanson. Armour started advertising its canned meat products as "TV Meals" in the mid-1950s, while Dupont introduced a premade "TV Dessert" of cake, ice cream, and berries. TV Time Popcorn even appropriated the movie theater's defining snack for home entertainment.[27] Then in 1962, Swanson dropped the name "TV Brand Dinner" from their frozen meals, ostensibly because they wanted to encourage consumers to eat frozen meals in other contexts. By then, the concept of the TV dinner had become so entrenched in American consumer culture that Swanson no longer needed the name anyway. Americans were so accustomed to eating in front of the television that they scarcely needed additional encouragement to do so.

\*     \*     \*

Although TV dinners and remote controls both contributed to mid-century television culture, it must be noted that the former were far more popular than the latter. *Television Digest* named remote controls the most popular television accessory in 1960, remote control remained an aspirational norm rather than a reality for most viewers. Only 10 percent of new television sets sold in 1961 had built-in remote controls, and that percentage actually fell over the rest of the decade.[28] In truth, remote controls did not become a common household appliance until infrared remotes took off in the 1980s. Yet even if few Americans actually owned ultrasonic remote controls, those devices still changed cultural perceptions of the technology. It was the ultrasonic's internal hammers that earned remote controls the nickname "the clicker." *Clicker* connotes novelty and affection but not necessity or power; as a nickname, it suggests that remote controls weren't held in high esteem during the 1960s. Despite advertisers' best efforts, consumers did not perceive themselves as needing remote controls, nor could the remote's conveniences outweigh its hefty price tag. Consequently, remote control development largely stagnated during the 1960s while manufacturers focused on producing smaller "portable" sets (with and without remote control). Ads for these smaller consoles reflected the prosperity and vitality of the early 1960s while their design reveals a move away from the old television-as-furniture aesthetic.

There was one 1960s remote control innovation that did have important ramifications for the future of television design, however. In 1961 RCA Victor introduced a color television set tuned primarily via remote control.[29] The remote's design was not particularly inspired: two rows of white push-buttons on a brown plastic and metal box the size of a pack of playing cards. What matters is that that device was the main interface for the set, which had no external tuning knobs or buttons. It did have a control drawer hidden above one of its speakers, but that panel was itself modeled after the Wireless Wizard (see figure 15). In fact, it was basically a remote control built into the side of the TV. RCA's design suggests that remote control was no longer just an accessory in the company's eyes: the remote had become an integral component of the television itself.

*　　*　　*

A little over a decade later, cable television would make remote control an integral component of viewer's lives by creating what Brian Winston calls a "supervening social necessity" for the device.[30] During the 1970s, a number of technological

FIGURE 15 Frame grab from "Television Remote Control (Tuner)" (circa 1961), a filmed advertisement for RCA Victor's Wireless Wizard remote-controlled television sets.

and industrial changes enabled cable providers to offer more channels and subscribers needed help managing these new channels easily and efficiently. Communications historian Patrick R. Parsons states the problem quite succinctly:

> There was an obvious drawback, for the consumer, to the increasing number of cable channels. Through thirty years of television, the happy, complacent viewer could and did sit through the evening watching one or perhaps two networks. The need to change channels during the evening was minimal. … The expanding choice of cable, however, means a decreasing ability to know what was on each channel at any given time.[31]

Cable gave viewers the opportunity to change channels more often, and that created a practical need for remote controls.

Technically, cable television began in the United States in 1948, but it only became a popular alternative to broadcast television after it took its modern form—as a subscription service for specialty and premium programming—in 1975. Before that, cable was known as Community Antenna Television (CATV) and its purpose was to amplify feeble broadcast signals for viewers in rural or geographically isolated communities.[32] Giant CATV antennas brought in stations too weak or distant for viewers to receive with home antennas. CATV providers amplified these signals and delivered them to subscribers through networks of coaxial cables. Consequently, CATV programming was no different than what most Americans caught over the airwaves, nor was it intended to be. CATV's business model changed in 1975, the year that HBO inaugurated national satellite delivery for premium cable channels. HBO revised providers' and viewers' expectations for cable programming with their successful nationwide transmission of the Mohammed Ali–Joe Frazier "Thrilla in Manila" fight that October. HBO proved that nationwide satellite broadcasting was commercially feasible and that viewers would pay more for premium sporting events and films, especially if such broadcasts were not interrupted by commercials. Local cable operators responded quickly, adding new national and specialized channels to their lineups. Channels like TBS, ESPN, and the Christian Broadcast Network helped differentiate cable from broadcast television, rendering it more valuable to more consumers.

Satellite transmission made these new national networks possible and thus contributed directly to the success of cable television and of remote controls. Before satellite, cable companies had to either "bicycle" (i.e., physically transport) tapes of their programs to their affiliates or transmit them over telephone lines rented from AT&T. Bicycling and telephone transmission were expensive and inefficient means to build national networks, which was the dream of cable moguls like Ted Turner and entertainment conglomerates like Time Inc., the money behind HBO.[33] Satellite transmission also helped specialty networks supply additional programming for cable providers, who were improving their home delivery protocols to offer more channels for subscribers. At the same time, the Federal Communications Commission revised its restrictions on cable programming to allow more direct competition between cable and broadcast stations. This regulatory change facilitated further centralization, corporatization, and growth in the cable industry throughout the 1970s.[34] By 1980, cable providers could offer viewers up to twenty-eight channels—an unprecedented abundance of choice—in bundles of basic and premium stations.[35] Cable was then in over 21 percent of US homes, and by 1990 it had penetrated almost 60 percent of US homes, with 90 percent of those homes receiving thirty channels or more.[36] It might have seemed extravagant to buy a remote control to switch between a handful of broadcast networks in the 1950s, but by the 1980s cable's relative cornucopia all but required remote control.

The 1970s cable converter remotes were gigantic, typically about half the size of a set-top converter box (see figure 16). Like the radio receiver remotes of the 1920s and 1930s, they were designed to be stationary chair-side tuning stations. Jerrold was among the first electronics manufacturers to produce cable converters with *wired* remotes. These devices typically came equipped with twelve buttons, one for each of the channels that cable providers were capable of offering at the time.[37] As Jerrold's remotes became more powerful, moreover, they only became larger. Once Jerrold added a UHF mode to its cable remote, for instance, the device reached the size of a full-scale computer keyboard. All

**FIGURE 16** A mid-1970s remote control for a Jerrold set-top cable converter box. Photo used by permission of John S. Flack, Jr

those buttons made cable converters easy to tune, but they prohibited manufacturers from offering wireless remote controls since ultrasonic remotes (still the best wireless remote control technology at the time) were not capable of enough frequency combinations for channel-specific tuning. Fortunately, the competitors' remotes were no smaller; Hamlin Electronics, for instance, offered a slide-scale cable converter remote with the dimensions of a hardback book. Early cable converter remotes made channel surfing possible, then, but only by compromising the remote's portability. While mid-century television remotes were all handheld, cable converter remotes reverted to a tabletop design.

They presumed that a viewer intended to stay in her easy chair, not go gallivanting around the house with her remote control. They also reveal something disingenuous about wireless remote control design. Although most wireless remotes have a high degree of motility—meaning they feel highly portable—we use them precisely so that we do not have to move at all. They emphasize motility and activity in order to make us feel less sedentary and passive while we use them.

*       *       *

At the same time that cable was giving us one reason to "need" remote control home video provided another. In 1975, Sony introduced Betamax, the first half-inch videocassette recorder—commonly known as the VCR—that allowed users to record television programs for subsequent viewing. VCRs fundamentally changed the nature of home entertainment. Viewers were no longer limited to watching whatever happened to be on at a given moment. Now they could choose between watching live TV, a previously recorded show, or commercially released prerecorded cassettes. VCRs gave television viewers unprecedented control over their media consumption, the ability to watch what they wanted when they wanted, to paraphrase an early Betamax ad. These viewers did not necessarily want to get up to program their new VCRs, however. So as Betamax and VHS fought to monopolize the video marketplace, remote control became a potential advantage each tried to leverage over the other—although ultimately VHS won for reasons that had little to do with remote control or any other technological advantage.[38]

As with cable converters, VCR remotes began as wired attachments. Sony started offering VCR remotes in 1979 as accessories for its higher-end Betamax units. Some of these early Betamax remotes possessed only a single function, namely pause. *Pause* was arguably the most revolutionary features of VCR viewing, which explains why it was the first to appear on a remote. Before pause, television viewers had no way to modify broadcasters' schedules. Imagine organizing your life around a television program; the inconvenience is almost inconceivable today! Before VCRs and digital video recorders (DVRs), viewers had to plan their bathroom and snack runs around television's commercial breaks. If the telephone rang, their only choice was to ignore it or miss an irrecoverable part of the show. The VCR and its pause button gave viewers control over the temporality of television, as did *fast-forward* and *rewind*. Never before had viewers been able to manipulate films or television shows to suit their preferences. At long last, the ability to interrupt the show when we wanted to! And Betamax's pause-only remote put this power in the hands of the viewer.

Within a year, Sony dramatically increased the functionality of VCR remotes with its Time Commander. The Time Commander featured not only pause, fast-forward, and rewind but also variable scan speeds and a Frame-By-Frame advance option. Ads for this new device promised Betamax consumers "the freedom of total control" (see figure 17).[39] "Freedom" is a peculiar word to attach to a remote control, especially a wired remote control that tethers its user to his VCR. Here it implies both freedom of choice (e.g., controlling video playback) and freedom from some prior constraint, presumably life before remote control. Although the promise of "total control" is as old as the remote control itself, Sony makes it new by pairing it with an oddly portentous picture of a man silhouetted in white light, holding a Time

**FIGURE 17** "The power to alter the fabric of time itself": A 1980 advertisement for Sony's Betamax "Time Commander" remote control.

Commander aloft in his right hand. The photograph doesn't attempt to hide the wire emerging from the top of the Time Commander, but it is difficult to tell where the wire leads. Does it disappear behind the man's arm or into it? At first glance, the Time Commander appears to be wired directly into its owner, so he appears to be some kind of cyborg time commander. Yet his Eames chair and the library of leather-bound books behind him suggest that the time commander is also a man of culture, an aesthete. The time commander is thus the perfect synthesis of 1980s high-tech, high-culture yuppie style.

Although Sony tried to present its wired remote as a defining component of the 1980s technochic lifestyle, the remote control itself had yet to become fully modern. That is, it had yet to find the technological platform proper to its aspiration of rebranding physical passivity as mental activity and control as power. A remote on a wire still looked (and sometimes felt) like a tether, and ultrasonics, though convenient, limited the number of commands a remote control could perform. It was not until the introduction of infrared LEDs in 1980 that remote controls fully realized the aspirations attached to them. Infrared remotes were capable of transmitting far more commands than ultrasonics with less interference for a fraction of the price. Ironically, infrared remotes employ the same basic medium as Zenith's ill-fated Flash-Matic remote: light. But whereas the Flash-Matic used full-spectrum light and four photocells, infrared remotes typically use one light-emitting diode (LED) to send coded flashes of long-wave electromagnet radiation (i.e., invisible infrared light) to a single photocell. RCA Labs created the first infrared LED in 1955, but Texas Instruments did not begin producing them for laboratory and electronics equipment until the early 1960s. These first-generation diodes sold for up to $260 each, so there was hardly any commercial market for the technology at first.[40] The price of infrared LEDs dropped precipitously over the next decade, however, until they cost as little at five cents apiece by the mid-1970s.[41] At that point, manufacturers could afford to integrate them into consumer electronics without substantially raising retail prices. The first infrared remote control was introduced by Canadian cable company Viewstar, in 1980; by 1985, infrared remotes had proven cheap and effective enough to supplant all other remote control technologies.

Most infrared remotes work by means of light-based binary codes known as pulse coding. The remote's LED transmits rapid flashes of light that the receiver decrypts based on either (a) the presence or absence of light at given intervals, (b) the length of time between pulses, or (c) the length of a given light pulse. When the user pushes a button on an infrared remote, it triggers the LED to send a signal comprised of:

- a start code (which tells the receiver a command is coming)

- a command code (which specifies the function to be performed)

- an address code (which identifies the receiver that should perform the command)

- a stop code (which lets the receiver know the command-address sequence is over)

The receiver has to "recognize" its address code before it can convert the command code into electrical impulses and perform the designated function. Address codes keep receivers from obeying the wrong remote controls, and—as I explain in the next chapter—they also make it possible for one remote to address more than one receiver, as in the case of universal remotes.

Because infrared technology was so affordable, manufacturers added infrared remotes to their less expensive television sets, cable boxes, and VCRs. In a sense, then, infrared LEDs democratized remote control, finally making the aspirational norm a common household gadget. Between 1984 and 1988, the penetration of remote controls in US television households doubled, from 33 percent to 66 percent.[42] By the early 1990s, infrared remotes were included with all kinds of consumer electronics, including CD players, stereos, air conditioners, and even gas fireplaces. Today, most American households have four or more remote controls in their living room.[43] The remote control turned out to be the little gadget that could … and did.

\*　　\*　　\*

As people started buying and using more home media devices, though, they needed better systems for organizing all their electronics, not to mention their remotes. For many, such "electronic sprawl" was epitomized by an overabundance of remote controls.[44] Many consumers tried to manage the mess with entertainment centers, an old concept reborn for the age of multiple set-top boxes. Since their invention in the 1910s, entertainment centers were designed to systematize and manage new media technologies by following one of two conflicting aesthetic principles: concealing electronics and displaying electronics. Many historians credit Frank Lloyd Wright with designing the first entertainment center as part of his Hollyhock House. Built in 1919, the Hollyhock House contains a dedicated "entertainment room" with built-in cabinets to exhibit radio and phonograph equipment and store LP records. In the 1950s, as television and the Space Age revived interest in the high-tech home, a 1951 issue of *American Home* showcased an especially well-appointed entertainment room (referred to as "*the room*") that "included a television set, radio, phonograph, movie projector, movie screen, loud speakers, and even a barbeque pit."[45]

There are also precedents for the entertainment center as freestanding furniture. In the 1920s, the media-as-furniture design trend described in Chapter 1 generated radio-phonograph "entertainment centers" like the Stromberg-Carlson Telektor. Radio-phonograph cabinets set a precedent for uniting multiple media devices within a single console, but the cabinets themselves also manifested the entertainment room's conflicting impulses toward exhibiting and hiding electronics. On the one hand, bringing multiple audio technologies together behind one stylish walnut façade helped to integrate them into living room décor. On the other hand, these multi-device consoles were gigantic pieces of furniture, so it seems unlikely that they ever really blended in. For postwar homeowners, a new trend toward portable television sets facilitated more modest versions of these entertainment hubs. Many so-called "portable" television sets were too heavy or too burdened with set-top boxes to really go anywhere, but because they were freestanding—that is, not contained within a floor console—furniture manufacturers could offer cabinets and armoires designed to organize, contain, and even hide media technologies in the modern living room.

Such entertainment centers serve both a practical and an ideological function. They make it easier to keep track of a television's many ancillary and accessory components—from cable converters to external speakers, remote controls to video game cartridges—and they express our attitudes toward the mass media. Some models, often known as television stands, display their devices as commodity fetishes; they present electronics as products to look at and appreciate even when not in use. Media armoires, on the other hand, promise to hide such devices from the domestic scene. By "closeting" the television, they turn your media habit into a dirty secret. Some television stands and media armoires include small drawers for remote controls, while others encourage owners to leave their remotes out as part of the technological display. Although home theaters replaced entertainment centers as a cutting-edge design trend in the late 1980s and 1990s, the entertainment center's basic principle—to bring all electronics together where they can be fetishized or concealed—continues to determine modern attitudes toward the high-tech home. In fact in 2012, IKEA returned the entertainment center to its media-as-furniture roots with the Uppleva, a side table with a built-in LCD TV, Blu-ray player, and 2.1 speaker system (some assembly required). Despite the Uppleva's streamlined design, IKEA's bold reinvention of the pre-equipped entertainment center ultimately failed. Its design garnered universal praise but the Uppleva's media components disappointed both reviewers and consumers. Its confusing, dual-layer remote control was just one such let-down, but it helped to prove that entertainment centers are only as good as the media devices they contain.[46]

*　　*　　*

In 1955 it was rare to find a television remote in any American living room; by 1985 it was rare to find just one. Satellite communications, cable converters, VCRs, and infrared LEDs all made remote controls a necessity for modern home media. Once viewers started using their television sets not only to view broadcast programming but also to watch cable channels and prerecorded videos and record television programs (not to mention play video games), those sets became hubs for entertainment systems that required a complicated arsenal of remote controls.

Within thirty years, then, remote controls went from convenience to necessity to clutter. By 1988, 63 percent of US households had at least one remote control; as of 1992, that number had surged to 84 percent.[47] Today it seems that the more remote controls a person has, the more likely it is that any given remote control will go missing the moment it's needed. As my friend Jeff puts it, losing a remote induces a kind of "existential bewilderment" by forcing us to acknowledge how dependent we are on these little gadgets.[48] The proliferation of remote controls also complicates their already paradoxical portability, since many of us now find ourselves tethered to not just one remote, but five or six. Remote clutter reminds us that control is not just a privilege; it can also be a burden. Many of my friends now write their own "dummy guides" to help guests navigate their remotes, and they are hardly alone.[49] Whereas families in the 1960s once fought over who got to hold the remote, some twenty-first century families fight for the right *not* to be in charge of the remotes. Today, the real luxury of remote control might be limiting one's exposure to them.

As remote controls proliferated, then, they betrayed many of the fantasies and aspirations initially attached to them. History has shown that remotes will not silence your wife, restore your masculinity, or bestow upon you "the freedom of total control." They helped usher in new cultural norms for American masculinity, home furnishings, and television consumption, but now we tend to regard them as irritants rather than historical agents. Remote controls are no longer a luxury but a nuisance. They frustrate rather than excite us. Manufacturers have responded to our frustration with two solutions: branded remotes and universal remotes. As I explain in the next chapter, both promise the user full dominion over the living room but demand some corporate loyalty in exchange. They can also be incredibly confusing, which changes the power dynamics of the modern living room. These multifunction devices reveal that the ease, luxury, and convenience of remote control are not necessarily empowering. If we let the remote teach us one thing, let it be this: power is a separate issue from control, and it has little to do with changing channels or muting commercials.

# 3 IT'S COMPLICATED

Every successful technology has its tipping point, the moment when it gains cultural momentum and goes from being "around" to being "everywhere." Sometimes that moment arrives quickly, as it did for DVD, the most rapidly adopted technology in the history of consumer electronics. Sometimes the moment never arrives, as in the case of Smell-O-Vision or any of the other entrepreneurial schemes cinema owners tried to help patrons "smell" the action on screen. For the remote control, that moment was the mid-1980s. Remotes were very expensive in the 1960s and 1970s, and their limited powers failed to justify the price for many consumers. Infrared LED technology brought that price down while other new media technologies (including satellite communications, cable television networks, and home video players) made remote control feel more like a necessity than a luxury. In 1981, remotes were in just 16 percent of US homes.[1] They would be in 51 percent by 1987, and by 1989, they would reach over 72 percent penetration.[2]

If you were around in the 1980s, you probably remember how remotes seemed suddenly to be everywhere. During the early 1980s, manufacturers started adding them as standard accessories to color television sets, VCRs and Laserdisc players, cable converter boxes, and stereo systems. By the end of the decade, they also began to appear alongside air conditioners, ceiling fans, bathtubs, and even the occasional toilet.[3] In June 1993, the Electronics Industry Association estimated that there were over ninety-nine million television remotes operating in the United States, plus an additional 125 million VCR, CD player, and cable converter remotes.[4] By 2000, most American households possessed four or more remote controls.[5] Remote controls were no longer an aspirational norm. They had become a fact of life.

As remote controls proliferated, though, their conveniences bred new inconveniences. The simple design of ultrasonic and radio remotes trained us to expect remote control to be straightforward. Those devices performed no more than a handful of commands, but they were at least easy to use. During the 1980s, lots of remotes with lots of remote-control buttons started creating lots of hassles. "The first remote in any household is a blessing," Ivan Berger observed in the *New York Times* in 1989. "The second is a joy, but as these blessings mount, they clutter up your coffee table—and the one you want always seems to be under a newspaper or the cat."[6] Berger suggested combatting clutter by "fastening a pair of remote controls back to back" to make one double-sided remote. Another home organizer recommended taping telephone wire to your remote controls so you could "plug" them into telephone jacks and tether them to the wall.[7] Their suggestions reveal that within ten years, remote controls had become a problem rather than a solution.

Part of the problem was that remote controls were now too complicated. In 1984 manufacturers started developing multifunction remotes that could control several media devices. The inherent complications of such gadgets frustrated many users. Berger's colleague Hans Fantel bemoaned the "hundred knobs, buttons and switches" on these "confusing controls," while Robert Adler—the inventor of the first ultrasonic television remote—joked that "given their complexity, perhaps you'll need a pilot's license" to use one, especially if you intend to program it to direct multiple components.[8] "The control experience of TVs has always been user-hostile," Casey Johnston recently grumbled in *Ars Technica*. "Modern remotes are littered with often inscrutable buttons ('sub.code'?), some with multiple functions ('comp/ mix'?), and only a few are used regularly. Multiply that by a remote for every component connected to your TV, and reading a book doesn't sound so bad after all."[9] Remotes were supposed to make electronics easier to control, but multifunction remotes violated that promise.[10] Remote control wasn't fun anymore; even its designers had to admit that it had become more torture than toy.

During the final decade of the twentieth century, remote control manufacturers scrambled to find a compromise between clutter and confusion, between too many dedicated single-device remotes and overly complicated multifunction remotes. They came up with three potential solutions: the branded multifunction remote, the universal multifunction remote, and the simplified secondary remote. The branded remote emerged first. In the mid-1980s, several electronics manufacturers introduced remote controls preprogrammed with address and command codes for a multiple products in their line. Within a year, independent remote control manufacturers also started selling "universal remote controls" that could "learn" the codes for any infrared-equipped media components. Branded and universal remotes were confusing to use, though, so in the early 1990s, a few electronics manufacturers started selling simplified secondary remotes to replace them.[11] These smaller, ergonomic remotes were capable of fewer commands than their multifunction equivalents. They included only the most popular commands, those originally associated with remote control, such as channel shifting and volume adjustment.

Sony's RM-K1T, for instance, could do little more than Adler's mid-century Space Command remote, but at least it only had nine buttons (see figure 18). Its limited functionality and simplified design appealed to viewers overwhelmed by the fifty-two buttons on Sony's other television remotes. Simplified remotes like the RM-K1T promised to resolve remote control confusion by limiting control, limiting the number of commands a user could perform. They also looked less complicated and easier to use, as their streamlined plastic shells belied the circuitry they contained. Through this sleight of hand, they made simplicity seem cutting edge when in fact media devices were becoming more complicated than ever

**FIGURE 18** A 1990 Sony RM-K1T remote control. Photo by author.

before. Simplified remotes were not a solution to the media's growing complexity, in other words. They were accessories people could buy to obscure that complexity and make the media feel user-friendly again.

Today Apple and Roku continue to use simplified remote control designs to make media convergence feel less overwhelming. Uniting movies, television shows, music, and web content in one device, they sooth consumers' fear of clutter and confusion by condensing a variety of media into one "black box." As media theorist Henry Jenkins explains, the black box is a design fantasy for total media convergence: "sooner or later, the argument goes, all media content [movies, television shows, music, and webpages] is going to flow through a single black box in your living room."[12] In 2010, Apple created a literal black box with its second-generation Apple TV, an impenetrable 4-inch-square black plastic block. The only way to program this media omnibus is with the Apple Remote, a slim aluminum wand that exemplifies simplified design. Its seven buttons place the wide world of digital media under your thumb without the confusion inherent to branded or universal remotes. The Apple Remote looks elegant and feels intuitive because Apple has realized that consumers are sometimes willing to pay for a device that both empowers them and helps them enjoy control.

It's ironic that the era of the remote control's greatest dominance is also the period when we began to understand it as a problem. As remote controls became more prevalent and powerful, users wanted to bring control itself under control. Too many remote controls with too many buttons gave us too much command, too much responsibility. Their replacements—branded and universal multifunction remotes and secondary remotes—reflect consumers' competing desires for more and simplified control, desires that generated a profound paradox for this moment in the device's history. Control has been both a luxury and a responsibility, but today we prefer to experience it as neither. Perhaps we would rather not think of our relationship with the media in terms of *control* at all anymore but instead in terms of *choice* or simply *cohabitation*. Those paradigms do not entail the same responsibility as control. Personally, even when such responsibility is limited to learning how to program one of my universal remotes, I would prefer not to. We don't want control to require anything of us, because then we might have to admit that the media requires something of us too. It requires us to be vigilant, to think, to ask whether it is operating in our best interests. Since the 1970s we have abbreviated *remote control* to *remote* arguably in order to disavow such duties. A *remote* promises physical and psychic distance from the media. It promises that we can remain inaccessible, removed, unharmed by the visions and voices we let into our lives. It's the same fantasy that inspired radio receiver remotes in the 1920s, the desire to sit back in our favorite easy chairs and just enjoy the show. Evidently, that fantasy still holds.

*       *       *

Manufacturers began developing branded multifunction remotes in the early 1980s in response to consumers' irritation with remote control clutter. These branded remotes were supposed to fight clutter by controlling multiple devices within a manufacturer's product line. Some people loved the innovation. Within two years of the branded remote's introduction, Hans Fantel praised it as "a complete interlinking of media … designed with an eye toward the future."[13] "An eye toward the future" indeed, because branded remotes were best at fighting clutter for consumers who didn't have clutter yet, who hadn't yet started buying the electronics that would bring remote controls into their lives. As other tech writers would point out, "by the time controller clutter becomes a problem, you are likely to have equipment and remote controls from several manufacturers."[14] Of course, manufacturers hoped that their consumers would just replace competitors' components once they bought a device with a branded remote, but that plan never proved popular. Talk about throwing the baby out with the bathwater—or rather throwing the VCR out just to get rid of its remote!

RCA was the first manufacturer to sell a branded remote control as a replacement for the annoying "half a dozen remote-control units cluttering your coffee table or making lumps on your bed."[15] Officially dubbed the "Dimensia Digital Control," this device was part of RCA's "ultimate home audio-video system," which they called Dimensia. When it was introduced in 1984, Dimensia's big selling point was that it used one remote to manage six components: an AM/FM radio, television set, VCR, and cassette, record, and CD players.[16] The television was the brain of the Dimensia network. Its infrared receiver and microprocessors could distinguish among the address and command codes for each component for the entire system. "The one remote does it all!" RCA crowed. And it should have, given that the Dimensia Digital Control boasted no less than fifty-two buttons (see figure 19). Its design was based on an earlier RCA remote, the Digital Command Center, which might technically have been the first branded multifunction remote except that

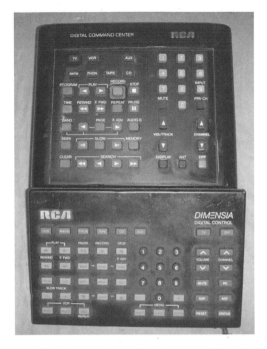

**FIGURE 19** "Total control" over "the theater of life": RCA's 1983 Digital Command Center and 1984 Dimensia Digital Control remote controls. Photo used by permission of Daniel Christensen.

it only worked with a few devices: RCA's Colortrak 2000 television set, SJT400 videodisc player, and a few VCRs. The Dimensia Digital Control, on the other hand, promised its user "total control" over "the theater of life."[17] "Theater of life" is a nice turn of phrase, but really the Dimensia system didn't offer its viewer any unique entertainment features or formats. It played the same radio stations, TV channels, videotapes, audio cassettes, records, and CDs as any other home-assembled entertainment center; it just happened to do all that using a single remote. The Dimensia Digital Control centralized powers previously dispersed among various media remotes into a single, seemingly all-powerful device. It put your whole home theater in the palm of your hand.

In other words, Dimensia's multifunction remote control made it easier to control multiple home entertainment devices than ever before. It promised to help its user command the ever-expanding universe of home media—provided she was willing to transform her house into an RCA fiefdom. In other words, that promise of "total control" was contingent upon total corporate loyalty. RCA emphasized the physical heft of these "total control" remotes in advertisements in order to make the power seem worth the price, which was nearly $7,000 for the full Dimensia system (or $16,028 today). In an early print ad for RCA's Digital Command Center, a female model grips the remote in both hands as though its weight and potency necessitated her full attention. Below the image, a small caption assures the reader that the illustration depicts the Digital Command Center in its "actual size." This is no mere "clicker"; the Digital Command Center looks more like a prototype for a personal digital assistant than a remote control. In fact it needs all those buttons to live up to the ad's copy, which called it, "the most impressive remote control you've ever laid hands on."[18] In this ad, RCA is trying to fetishize complexity for its own sake, to make the viewer value buttons whether those controls are useful or not.

By 1986, RCA's Dimensia system had inspired a field of imitators, including the Sony Access home theater, Technics' AV500 series, and Pioneer's Foresight 70 collection. These branded entertainment systems all included television sets, radios, VCRs, videodisc players, cassette and CD players, and even speakers and turntables. They could all be operated with a single remote control, but most were much less expensive than the Dimensia, retailing for as little as $3,290 (or $7,225 today). They still weren't cheap though; in fact, their high prices were intended to mark single-manufacturer entertainment systems as high-end. As Pioneer boasted in a 1986 ad for the Foresight 70, "It is possible to put the best of everything in one system. It's simply not easy."[19] Pioneer emphasized the efficiency of the Foresight 70's single multifunction remote, since as Hans Fantel insisted, "the best of everything" really ought to put "an end to the clutter and confusion of separate remote-control devices for the television set, the VCR and the stereo components." Like its competitors, the Foresight 70 perpetuated and obeyed the "sybaritic premise" that high-end electronics ought to require minimal physical effort from their users (after the initial set-up, of course).[20] Pioneer's ad actually reflects this logic; it wasn't easy for them to put together such as system, but it will be easy for you to use it. The remote control was a crucial part of this promise. Like the advertisements themselves, branded remotes helped give consumers the impression that the more expensive, complicated, and cutting edge a branded entertainment system is, the less effort it ought to require of them, including any effort to locate the remote. *If you're paying $3,300 for an entertainment center*, these multifunction remotes assured their users, *you shouldn't have to go hunting for a different remote for each and every component. How very plebeian!*

The 1980s branded entertainment centers were the beginning of "combined audio-video 'home theaters'" as a trend among American electronics consumers.[21] "Home theater" was not a new concept, but in the 1980s it gained popularity as shorthand for an integrated multimedia home entertainment system. In *Beyond the Multiplex*, Barbara Klinger recounts the evolving rhetoric of home theater, noting that the dream of an in-home cinema goes back at least as far as 1912.[22] Television advertisers, manufacturers, and enthusiasts employed the term for decades, first to celebrate television's potential as an art form and then to emphasize particularly elaborate or large-screen television set-ups.[23] But "fully integrated, single-brand audio-video combinations" like RCA's and Pioneer's marked a new understanding of home theater that wasn't restricted to TV. Within these systems, television was no longer "just television." Instead of being an autonomous broadcast medium, the set served as a "monitor-receiver" for many other audio-visual components, including VCRs, cable boxes, and videodisc players.[24]

The 1980s home theaters were typically much more elaborate than the entertainment centers of the 1960s and 1970s. For one thing, they often required—or were pictured as occupying—their own rooms. Gigantic television monitors necessitated that viewers watch from across the room, which made remote control a critical component of any home theater. Remember that "sybaritic premise": high tech means low effort. So improved remote control was essential to the home theater's appeal, namely "redefining the home as a site *par excellence* for media consumption," as Klinger puts it.[25] Manufacturers also suggested that home theater systems could improve consumers' social status. Their ads implied that owning a high-tech home theater would connote "particularly attentive viewing sensibilities and heightened sensory experiences." It would also demonstrate good taste, since recent "pervasive equations of technology itself with art" meant that media components were no longer just a means to reproduce music and film.[26] Properly designed, they too could achieve artistic distinction.

To be sure, the home theater movement continued to emphasize good sound fidelity and image resolution, but it also suggested that networking media devices could be an art in itself. Multifunction remote controls made the art of the network visible in a way that individual device control panels and remotes never could. Hence critics celebrated the Bang & Olufsen Beo5000 audio system for its monolithic design and computerized remote. A sleek tower of brushed aluminum and dark plastic, the Beo5000 had no visible interface. The only way to program it was through its remote, the Beo5000 Control Panel, which was the size of a small computer keyboard and featured an impressive built-in LED display. Like the Digital Command Center, the Beo5000 Control Panel stressed the remote control's entry into the digital age. Its rectangular shape and elaborate button grid implied that consumers should understand remotes as computerized, not mechanical, from then on.

*    *    *

Universal remotes also helped associate media technologies with personal computers because, like computers, they were programmable. They appealed to consumers who did not want to buy an entire home theater from a single manufacturer, people who already owned components made by different companies or who wanted to cherry-pick the right television monitor, videodisc player, VCR, and stereo. Because you could supposedly program them to control any infrared-equipped media device by any manufacturer, they were also known as "learning remotes" as well as universal remotes. The first learning remotes were sold as aftermarket accessories consumers could use in lieu of multiple single-device remotes, but by the mid-1990s many manufacturers included preprogrammed "universal" remotes with their media components. Preprogrammed remotes are never really universal, though, because they are only preprogrammed with a limited number of address and command codes. That said, most of the so-called universal remote you'll see on sale today are in fact preprogrammed rather than learning devices. The preprogrammed remote that comes with your new television or cable box *likely* contains the address and command coded for all the components in your home theater, but it does not necessarily contain them. If it doesn't, there's nothing you can do to reprogram it. "Learning" remotes, on the other hand, are truly universal because a user can—indeed must—program them. These devices tend to be more expensive than preprogrammed remotes, but some electronics enthusiasts also consider them more valuable, more impressive, because they require more technical prowess from their owners.

Steve Wozniak, the engineer behind the Apple I and Apple II computers, designed the first learning remote, the CL9 CORE (see figure 20). CORE stood for "Controller of Remote Equipment," a "universal programmable master remote" or "master controller" capable of mimicking the commands of any infrared remote control.[27] "Woz" designed the CORE around a MOS 6052 microprocessor, common to video game consoles of the era. The MOS 6052 allowed the CORE to "learn" new address and command codes while its 36KB memory enabled it to store those codes. But programmability was only one of the CORE's several advantages over contemporaneous branded remotes like the Dimensia Digital Control. The CORE could also simplify the remote control process, because users could assign a chain of commands to a single button. You could set one operating key to turn on the TV, tune it to a specific channel, and

**FIGURE 20** A CL9 CORE remote control from 1985. Photo used by permission of Ray Kester, K-Tronics, LC.

increase volume all at once. The CORE's built-in timer also enabled time-specific commands, including sleep modes, alarm functions, and multiple recording timers. No other 1980s remote could do that!

The problem was that first you had to program the CORE, which was no simple feat. The CORE only had six operating keys (labeled "a" through "f"), and each operating key could be assigned a different command for each "page" in the CORE's memory. Page one might control the television set, page two the VCR, and so on for up to sixteen pages. What each page and key combination did depend on how you programmed your CORE. Pressing the "a" key when the CORE was set to page one might turn the television on or off, while pressing the "a" key when the CORE was set to page two might start a CD or cue a preset radio station. It was entirely up to you. Users assigned commands to the CORE's operating keys using the programming keys contained in a second, hidden keyboard. Using this second keyboard, you would first have to enable CORE's learning mode and then choose a particular page and key to program. After that, you'd line the CORE up with another remote and press the key for your chosen command on that remote. The CORE would "capture" the other remote's infrared signal for that command and store it, so that whenever users entered that particular page and key combination thereafter, it issued the same infrared signal as the original remote. The CORE could store up to ninety-six page-key combinations, and its owner would have to "teach" it every one of those ninety-six commands, which could take hours, even days. For that reason, the CORE manual strongly encouraged owners to keep track of their programming choices in the "CORE journal" that came with the remote. That journal was probably very helpful when it came time to teach the rest of the family how to use their new remote!

Programming universal remotes has gotten a lot simpler since the days of CORE, but it is still a major hurdle for many of us. Today most preprogrammed remotes—the ones that come with our television sets, cable boxes, and videodisc players today—include a variety of different manufacturers' remote control commands already stored in their memory. We only need to inform these devices which components we want them to command, and yet somehow the process still seems overwhelming. In order to pair most preprogrammed remotes with a media component, you need to press and hold a function button (like *DVD* or *AUX*), which activates the remote's programming mode, then enter the component code for that device's manufacturer. Then voilà! The universal remote should start "speaking the language" of that device whenever it is in that function mode. True, there is sometimes more than one component code for a given electronics manufacturer listed in a remote's manual or on its manufacturer's website. In that case, you just need to keep trying each component code in turn until one works. The process isn't particularly complex, but it can prove tedious. As a result, few remote owners ever program their so-called preprogrammed remotes. There are no studies on the percentage of multifunction remote owners who program their remote controls to command multiple components, but before I started doing the research for this book, I confess that I never did. As much as I may hate remote control clutter—and I do hate it—I evidently fear remote control confusion even more.

I also suspect that as excited as we may be by the prospect of "smart remotes" and "smart homes," we also fear that such instruments will prove smarter than we are—or maybe that they'll prove how smart we're not. Because we change remote controls infrequently and the process of programming them is slightly different every time, it's hard to remember how to do it from one time to the next; it's difficult to form an intuitive understanding of these devices. Remote control designers tried to respond to this anxiety with "code search" or "autopairing" functions. These commands make programming universal remotes as simple as the push of a button. Instead of manually entering component codes (as described above), users keep pressing *Code Search* or *Power* over and over until the remote locates the right infrared code for any given device.[28] The process is rather like approaching a stranger on the street and saying "Hello!" in as many languages as you can think of until she says "Hello!" back. Autopairing can take a while, but eventually the remote will find the right code...assuming, of course, that its manufacturer included that code in the remote's memory. If not—if you own a particularly old or obscure television set or VCR—then you're out of luck. As mentioned, no preprogrammed "universal" remote is truly universal. Only learning remotes like the CORE deserve that title.

*       *       *

With so many functions and buttons generating so much confusion, branded and universal remotes presented major challenges for the electronics industry. Controlling more components requires more functions, which requires more buttons, yet studies show that the more buttons a remote has, the fewer buttons people actually use.[29] Even within the consumer electronics industry, many designers believed multifunction remotes were problematic because their design reflects the logic of their engineers rather than the needs of their users.[30] As Robert Adler told a *Los Angeles Times* reporter in 2004, "I think it's scandalous how little people who design these things seem to keep in mind that people don't know it by heart as they do."[31] Adler's comment reveals an age-old tension in industrial product development between product- or engineer-centered design and user-centered design.[32] Design theorists Donald R. Gentner and Jonathan Grudin explain that "From the engineer's perspective, the ideal interface reflects the underlying mechanism and affords direct access to the control points of the mechanism. …The user, however, wants to complete a task, and an interface that is based on the task is often more appropriate than one based on the system mechanism."[33] In other words, engineers and users have very different ideas about what constitutes the best approach to product design. Gentner and Grudin found that engineers hope a product will reflect how it works, while users want a product that "just works." They specifically cite the CORE remote control as a device that privileges its mechanism over usability. Although the CORE's page system and variable button assignments are difficult to learn, they do allow us users to become involved in the programming process rather than making decisions on our behalf. The CORE is complicated, then, because multifunction remote control is complicated. But users do not necessarily want to get involved in their remotes' integrated circuits or logical structure; most of the time they just want to change the channel or play a video. In the late 1980s and early 1990s, designers tended to ignore such task-oriented thinking in favor of branded and universal multifunction remotes that enabled maximum customization.

Consequently, the average 1990s multifunction remote featured thirty to fifty buttons, many of which brought up on-screen menus that required further navigation. Some of these buttons only performed one obscure command, such as moving the Picture-in-Picture window. *New York Times* reporter Edward Rothstein called these extraneous buttons "vestigial" because most users never try them.[34] They represent the logic of the engineer—or of a design team desperately seeking an advantage over the competition—but they have little to do with the needs of the viewer. Put simply, they enable a degree of control that exceeds most people's interest in control. In the early days of the multifunction remote, Hans Fantel once proposed that his readers "practice the commands for a couple of hours" whenever they got a new remote control so that they could take advantage of each and every button.[35] Practical advice, maybe, but who among us has ever followed it? I am not even sure it would improve our understanding of remote control, since there is some evidence that these vestigial buttons follow a logic even more primal than that of their designers', namely the logic of the market. In the 1990s, manufacturers discovered that consumers were so frustrated with vestigial buttons that they were willing to buy a second less complicated remote to avoid them. In short, bad design could be good for business.

Two particular remotes, the Sony RM-K1T and the Mitsubishi PRM-1, exemplify the design principles of the simplified remote: petite proportions and a bare minimum of controls. The Sony RM-K1T was the size of a credit card and had just nine buttons, only one of which triggered an on-screen menu. It performed only a few basic commands, such as channel shifting and volume adjustment, but it definitely delivered a streamlined user experience; finally, for the first time in years, a remote that looked and felt easy to use! Also, the RM-K1T's pliable plastic bubble buttons were part of the card's skin. They rebound under your finger, making the RM-K1T feel solid and simple, almost anti-technological, by belying the circuitry hiding beneath them. Mitsubishi's PRM-1 was even sleeker, boasting a mere three buttons on its "pen-shaped" frame (see figure 21).[36] These buttons—power on/off, channel up/down, and volume up/down—are not even labeled. The PRM-1's designer, Doug Patton, shaped each differently so that users could distinguish them by feel. In fact the PRM-1 might be the first remote control devised so that users wouldn't have to look at it to use it. Patton's peers awarded the PRM-1 a gold medal for electronics design at the Industrial Design Excellence Awards, although they also acknowledged that a completely cylindrical remote has its shortcomings, namely that it can "be hard to find and might roll off the table."[37]

**FIGURE 21** A 1990 Mitsubishi PRM-1 remote control. Photo by author.

Patton's next simplified remote solved these problems and made it into the Museum of Modern Art. In 1995, his Palm-Mate universal remote control was part of the museum's exhibit "Mutant Materials in Contemporary Design." Introduced by Go-Video in June 1993, the Palm-Mate looked like a cross between a flying saucer and a wad of "squashed Silly Putty."[38] Featuring a mere seven buttons, it fit neatly into the palm of your hand so that you needed only rock your thumb back and forth or side to side to change channels, adjust volume, or control video playback (see figure 22). *Business Week* and *Wired* immediately heralded the Palm-Mate's clever ergonomic shape as "a joy to hold"

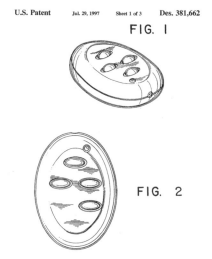

FIG. I

FIG. 2

**FIGURE 22** An illustration from Doug Patton's US patent application for the Palm-Mate remote control.

and one of the most important design innovations of the year.[39]

Patton designed the Palm-Mate for both usability and comfort because Go-Video needed it to be both easier to program and easier to hold than the remotes they sold with their signature dual-deck VCR. That device, the VCR-2, was designed to facilitate tape-to-tape home dubbing, and in 1993 it was the product Go-Video was most known for, in part because they'd sued seventeen different major Japanese electronics manufacturers for refusing to produce it.[40]

As you might imagine, the VCR-2's multifunction remote control was a design nightmare, one of the button-bedecked "monochromatic slices of hard plastic" that gave 1990s remotes a bad reputation.[41] It even came with a half-hour video tutorial, which did nothing to make the device seem more user-friendly. Go-Video hired Patton to design a simplified aftermarket remote for VCR-2 owners to pick up when they just wanted to watch a movie. After some field research, Patton came to the conclusion that ideally "you shouldn't have to move your finger from button to button" while using a remote. He also decided that a remote should feel as comfortable in the hand as "rounded stones at the beach."[42] The result was the Palm-Mate. Patton's hypothesis proved correct: test users loved their Palm-Mates. They fondled the devices like worry stones, so Go-Video ended up having to refabricate the Palm-Mate out of more durable materials. Perhaps because of their enthusiasm, the company also decided to alter Patton's original design and make the Palm-Mate into a universal remote. Early sales were unprecedented—Go-Video sold almost 10,000 Palm-Mates in their first forty-five days on market. Then the fad petered out, or maybe the Palm-Mate still wasn't tough enough to withstand all that love. At any rate, these peculiar remotes have become almost impossible to find today.

At the same time that Go-Video was championing the Palm-Mate, Sony introduced another funny looking ergonomic remote control: the RM-VP1 Remote Commander, colloquially known as the "Air Egg." No bigger than a cat toy (and about as easy to lose), the Air Egg was a marvel in remote design. It looked like a black chicken egg with a button on one side, but it was actually a wireless radio transmitter. The Air Egg worked with a specially arranged antenna to control the cursor for on-screen menus in Sony's STR-G1ES "Vision Touch" home theater set-up. Once all the other STR-G1ES components were in place, all a user needed to do was pick up the Air Egg, place her thumb over its single button, and move it left or right to guide the cursor. Using radio technology, then, Sony created the first graphic user interface for remote control. It allowed users to point and click through the Vision Touch menu to cue various devices in the STR-G1ES network. However, an improperly installed antenna or interference between the Air Egg and its antenna could compromise the entire Vision Touch system. Users were also frustrated by the system's complicated menus, not to mention a "mouse" that was nowhere near as sensitive as the wired mice they'd grown accustomed to using with their personal computers. Sony discontinued the Vision Touch system within a couple of years but it continued to experiment with egg-shaped remote controls through the mid-1990s, including the RM V30 "wobble action" universal remote. "Wobble action" was a bit of misnomer, though, because the wobble didn't do anything. The RM V30 was just an egg-shaped preprogrammed universal remote with a weighted base. RM V30s are still around, and still curious-looking, but like the Air Egg, the Palm-Mate, and other simplified 1990s remotes, they demonstrate that novely alone could not solve the problems of remote control clutter and confusion. Designers still had to figure out how to make a full-function multifunction remote that users did not resent using.

*   *   *

Although the era of simplified secondary remotes lasted no more than a few years, devices like the Palm-Mate and the RM V30 started a trend toward ergonomic remote control design. Ever since the mid-1950s, when Zenith replaced the Lazy-Bones bullet and the Flash-Matic "flash gun" with the Space Command box, remote controls had been basically rectilinear. Any given remote might be the size of a hardback book or a slim as a credit card, but they all relied on straight lines and right angles. The simplified ergonomic remotes of the 1990s encouraged designers to consider other alternatives. Between the late 1990s and early 2000s, rounded corners, tapered waists, and convex bottoms would become more common among second-generation multifunction remotes. These remotes blended the tactile pleasures of ergonomic design with the button grids necessary for multifunction control. They all followed one breakthrough device: the TiVo Peanut.

When industrial designer Paul Newby developed the Peanut for TiVo in July 1998, there was nothing like it on the market. Nor was there anything like TiVo, which was the first successful digital video recorder (DVR) in the United States. At first, TiVo's founders considered supplying a generic universal remote with their DVR units, but later the company asked Newby to create a unique and eye-catching TiVo control, "a remote that grabbed attention off the coffee table." Newby decided that such a remote also needed to be physically user-friendly, "comfortable for long periods of in-hand use."[43] For over eight and a half months, Newby and his team experimented with a series of oblong prototypes whose key design could accommodate single-handed control. Their remote would be the antithesis of hefty 1980s remote-control keyboards like the Dimensia Digital Control.

That device, "the Peanut," had a pleasingly organic-seeming shape that also conveniently emphasized TiVo's DVR controls, those capabilities that made TiVo more than just another cable converter box. Those buttons—*play*, *pause*, *fast-forward*, and *rewind*—were located at the device's waist, directly under the user's thumb. The directional keys for navigating TiVo's on-screen menus were positioned in the remote's second-most ergonomic spot, right in the middle of its higher bulb, so that users could still manipulate them with one thumb if they gripped the remote slightly higher up. Meanwhile the numerical keypad occupies the bottom of the remote. That awkward location makes it difficult to use the Peanut's number keys with just one hand, yet it still demonstrates good user-centered design. Newby assumed that TiVo viewers were unlikely to manually enter channel numbers when they could simply scroll through the service's interactive programming guide. They needed easy access to directional keys so they could move up and down between channels and laterally between time periods, but numerical keys could be harder to reach because viewers probably wouldn't enter channel numbers numerically as often. Following that logic, Newby hypothesized that channel surfing would be less frequent among TiVo users, so his team moved the Peanut's channel-shift button off center and slightly above the user's natural thumb position. As a result, the Peanut was not only easier to hold than other multifunction remotes, it was also better suited for a new era of television menus.

The Peanut's shape and layout brought it multiple awards from the Consumer Electronics Association. They also inspired many imitators. Remote control manufacturers began producing all sorts of rounded obelisks and oblongs (see figure 23). While most rectilinear remotes tended to be evenly thick from top to bottom, these rounded post-Peanut remotes are not. They tend to be bottom-heavy, which creates a lower and more agreeable center of gravity when held in the hand. Their tapered waists also enable a firmer grip for your index finger, which expands the thumb's

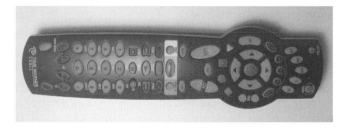

**FIGURE 23** A 2008 Universal Electronic Atlas UCAP universal remote control. Photo by author.

range of motion. And while rectilinear remotes typically used evenly sized and spaced buttons, post-Peanut remotes vary their buttons' colors, shapes, and spacing. These changes make it easier to use our remotes without looking at them. That said, post-Peanut remotes rarely have any fewer buttons than their predecessors, and their "universal" features aren't any easier to program. Because they physically feel more user-friendly, though, they still offer a more enjoyable user experience. For Doug Patton, the old boxy multifunction remotes felt "like Chinese water torture" because while no one task was all that difficult to execute, none were easy, which created an overall sense of user-hostility.[44] Ergonomic remotes offer the opposite experience. They seem like tools designed to help us negotiate the ever-expanding world of home entertainment.

Most of these design innovations began with the Peanut but one predates it: the D-pad, which arose from a curious convergence between remote controls and video game controllers. Directional pads or D-pads first appeared on remote controls in the 1990s as replacements for the jog/shuttle dials often featured on high-end 1980s VCR and Laserdisc remotes. Jog/shuttle dials allowed VCR users to rewind or fast-forward through cassettes at variable rates of speed—a handy feature for video editors but unnecessary for everyday viewers. The real advantage of jog/shuttle dials was that they looked cool. Their mere presence implied connoisseurship and technological sophistication. So when manufacturers began phasing the dials out, they continued to offer circular configurations of buttons. Often such button-circles comprised the playback buttons—play, fast-forward, stop, and rewind—but as on-screen menus became more popular, the D-pad joined playback button wheels on nearly all universal remotes. On most video game controllers, D-pads are either circular (as in the case of the first D-pad, designed for Mattel's Intellivision game system in 1979) or cross-shaped (as in the case of Nintendo's "+ control pad" introduced in 1985). They help players navigate multi-dimensional screen space, and they would prove ideal tools for navigating the menu interfaces then becoming popular among digital media platforms.

For instance, D-pads would turn out to be both a symptom of and catalyst for major changes in the way Americans figured out what to watch on TV in the twenty-first century. They help us engage the interactive electronic program guide (EPG) that defines the digital cable experience, but they also encouraged cable providers to adopt interactive EPGs. The first EPGs were scrolling grids of channel listings. The United Video Satellite Group started offering scrolling EPGs for some US cable providers as early as 1991; by 1996, StarSight Telecast was providing the service for most Viacom, Time Warner, and Cox Cable subscribers.[45] Although few were willing to pay four dollars a month to watch real-time station listings, once they were bundled into standard cable packages, scrolling EPGs quickly replaced printed television listings as viewers' preferred televisual reference system. The first patent for an interactive EPG was filed in 1988, but the concept did not become a televisual reality until after 1998, when digital cable delivery exponentially increased the number of stations viewers could receive. Scrolling EPGs were impractical, even annoying, when you had to wait for them to work through hundreds of channels. Many industrial designers weighed in on the best way to present searchable television listings to cable customers. They worried that complicated stacked-menu interfaces might frustrate older viewers, even if they were accurate in representing digital cable as a database of television shows rather than a stream of programming. In 1998, *Design Week* characterized the issues facing interactive EPG as an ideological conflict between "the linear presentation of TV listings" and the complexity of cyberspace. Ultimately they concluded that in the new information age, "navigation is spatial, selection is linear," and TV viewers needed remote controls that could help them exert control across both paradigms.[46]

The D-pad was not the only option for navigating digital TV—as Sony's Air Egg and WebTV's keyboard can demonstrate—but it was one of few remote control innovations that actually helped viewers approach television as information, perhaps because historically, television viewers have proven averse to any interface that demands additional physical or mental activity from them. Keyboard-based controllers like those offered by WebTV, MSN TV, and Google TV keep failing because their rows of keys require too much visual and mental attention and interrupt viewers' regularly scheduled relaxation. As long as viewers "want to munch dinner while they interact," *Design Week* predicts, we are going to see "mouse and keyboard ... rejected [by users and designers] as a messy interface solution."[47] Keyboards remind us of work rather than play—and take it from me, it's hard to eat popcorn and type at the same time. Fortunately, the D-pad's directional keys make it easy for viewers to peruse interactive EPGs with one hand while eating with the other, and they don't offend or confuse older viewers.

Along with interactive EPGs, DVD players provided a second major impetus for integrating D-pads into universal remote controls. Introduced in 1997 as a replacement for VHS and Laserdisc, DVD was the first home video format to bundle films and television shows with previews, deleted scenes, documentary featurettes, and other bonus materials that viewers could access through on-screen menus. DVD was the first home video platform to offer D-pads in its remote controls. VHS and Laserdisc did not need to offer viewers four-way control, after all, since their content could only be navigated in two (e.g., forward and backward). So was until the late 1990s that menu-based digital media like DVD, digital cable, and DVD made D-pads a standard element of remote control design. Thereafter, D-pads became so *de rigueur* for remotes that when Apple introduced its streamlined Apple Remote in 2007, they did away with basically every convention of remote control design except the D-pad!

\*       \*       \*

For better or worse, the Apple Remote marks the return of the branded remote to US consumer electronics. It combines the streamlined appeal of simplified secondary remotes with the menu-based interactivity of modern multifunction remotes. The first-generation Apple Remote was a thin white plastic bar less than two inches long. It came with the company's 2005 universal iPod dock so that people playing their iPod on a television set or computer could change songs or videos without crossing the room. Its design borrowed heavily from the first-generation iPod shuffle, specifically the layout of its menu button and central play/pause button surrounded by a directional wheel. In March 2007, Apple also began including remotes with the new Apple TV, and six months later—when a software upgrade transformed the Apple TV into a stand-alone iTunes store for your television set—the Apple Remote became the Apple TV's only control interface.

This design decision matters because in many ways the Apple TV is the closest any manufacturer has come to the proverbial black box: a single set-top box that streams all types of media. With its second-generation release in 2010, the Apple TV became a literal black box, a visual pun for the media-theory geeks among us. One of the strengths of Apple's brand has always been their willingness to subordinate engineer- or product-centered design to user-centered design. The black box is the apotheosis of that principle; its shell purposefully obscures as much as possible about how it works so that we place absolute faith in its inner workings and (ideally) never question its design. Apple TVs do not work without Apple Remotes (or an iPhone Remote app, about which more later), and their design extends the black box's mystification. The 2009 second-generation Apple Remote looks like a cross between a tiny computer and a magic scepter (see figure 24). With its brushed aluminum shell and a balanced wheel-and-circle design, it's cool to the touch and pleasing to the eye. Most twenty-first-century remotes look as complex as corporate media conversion actually is—a mess of unevenly and semi-autonomous companies and genres coming together. But the Apple Remote is refreshingly simple. Its clean lines promise to transport us to a chic and well-ordered universe: that of the Apple brand itself.

Apple's Remote app extends this promise by transforming iPhones, iPads, and iPod Touches into remote controls—and remote control into a computer program. Introduced in 2008, the Remote app offers users the same navigational and control buttons as an Apple Remote but through a touch screen. It is one of hundreds of remote control applications today, most of which also recreate the basic design and layout of a remote control device for a touch-screen interface. In other

**FIGURE 24** A 2009 second-generation Apple Remote. Photo by author.

words—and despite what you might read elsewhere—remote apps are not reinventing remote control. From D-pads to double-arrow buttons for fast-forward and rewind, remote apps are all skeuomorphs. They use new technology to imitate old technology. From the Greek terms *skéuos* (meaning tool or container) and *morphé* (meaning shape), the term *skeuomorph* was coined by H. Colley March in 1890 to describe objects that retain elements of a preceding technology's design for purely ornamental reasons. The trash-can icon in a Macintosh's graphic user interface exemplifies the principle of skeuomorphism; so do the fake grill marks on a frozen veggie patty. They recall an older product—a waste-paper basket, grilled meat—because that reference is comforting or reassuring, not because these products actually have anything in common with their predecessors. Most remote control apps visibly resemble earlier remote control devices, so we don't have to worry about how a change in media technology might change the media we're consuming or what we take from it as consumers. If anything, they go out of their way represent themselves as part of the lineage of remote control rather than an alternative future. They harness new technology to recreate faithfully the design and function of an earlier technology, to reassure us that new media will be the "same as it ever was."

Skeuomorphs and black boxes might seem like antithetical trends in media design, but they are actually highly compatible because they both hide how a technology actually works to indulge the user in a fantasy about how it might work (or that it just works). Apple is the leading purveyor of both skeuomorph and black box design, but it is hardly the only one, especially in the case of black boxes. Roku introduced a competing line of set-top streaming media devices in September 2010, and other consumer electronics companies now follow this trend toward control panel-free, remote-dependent design. Take a look at your flat screen television set; does its façade feature any buttons, any controls at all? My current television, a 2007 Sony XBR, does have one panel of primary function buttons hidden on the top of the set, but the new Samsung 4K Ultra HD Smart TV that I'm eyeing does not. Instead it comes with a Smart Touch remote that responds to push-button or voice commands. Using voice command, I may not even need to touch my remote to use it. I will be remote from my remote, though the remote will remain an essential intermediary between me and the TV. Whereas remotes once gave users the option of controlling their TVs at a distance, now distance appears to be our only choice. It seems that when it comes to watching TV these days, remote control is no longer an accessory for the monitor. Rather the monitor is an expression of remote control.

*     *     *

Pundits enjoy suggesting that remote controls will disappear soon, that they will be replaced by smart phone apps or voice-command interfaces like the Xbox One with Kinect. Maybe—but the surest way to be wrong about the future is to predict it. Even if remote control devices one day evolve past the point of similarity with any of those described in this book, the concept of *remote control* will remain the same. Remote control makes our interaction with the media as ethereal as broadcast signals. Voice command only furthers that trend, although it is worth noting that—like Samsung— most manufacturers are adding voice command microphones to remote controls, not to the components themselves. Over the past thirty years, remote control designers and users have migrated between branded remotes, universal remotes, and simplified secondary remotes in their quest to manage the ever more complicated world of home entertainment. Their experiments—both the successes and the failures—attest to our desire to get a grip on the ever-expanding world of mass media: to bring it to hand, so to speak. The more invasive the media becomes, the more pervasive its presence in our lives, the more appealing the concept of remote control becomes. But we also want remote controls that feel controllable, that strike that delicate balance between necessary function and unwanted complication. There is no one perfect remote; ninety years of remote control innovation surely demonstrates that. In fact history suggests that *remote control* is really a Platonic ideal, only ever partially realized in this world. So we keep striving for it, building and buying new devices to approximate it. True remote control hovers just beyond our grasp, like a controller stuck beneath a couch cushion: so close and yet so far.

# AFTERWORD

lthough we tend to think of academics as shut off in a metaphorical ivory tower, far from the real world and real stuff, they have actually been studying stuff for a very long time. In the 1890s, anthropologists Émile Durkheim, Franz Boas, and Lewis Henry Morgan argued that material objects were capable of transmitting ideology between the people who made and used them and that these objects were also shaped by ideology—that is, by the network of ideas, beliefs, and norms that organize a society. Durkheim, Boas, and Morgan held that by studying a culture's artifacts, outsiders could learn a lot about the society, how its members interacted, and what they valued. In the 1970s, design historians extended these claims to include mass-produced commodities as well as handcrafts; they contended that industrially developed, factory-made objects also reveal important information about the cultures that create them. A Thermos has just as much to tell us about the man who uses it as a handmade drinking gourd. Today philosophers, sociologists, and even literature scholars agree: objects do not have to be artisanal in order to be meaningful.

Objects reflect the culture that produces them, and they also influence that culture. As we have seen, remote controls were shaped by the Victorian doctrine of separate spheres, but they also changed the way people interpreted that doctrine, what they decided would be appropriate for family life in the twentieth century. Remotes encouraged greater media consumption. They facilitated new forms of patriarchal control for the family's "electronic hearth," and they also inspired new ways of wasting time, like "channel surfing." Remote controls show us that material culture is about more than just what we do to objects; it's also about what objects do to us. Human beings may have invented remote controls, but when a remote control and a human come into contact, both are affected by that encounter. We make these gadgets, but they make us, too.

All the objects in an environment influence each other, whether that environment is the Sonoran desert or a suburban living room. In the latter case, radio loud speakers inspired remote control, and remote controls influenced the design of easy chairs, television sets, and living rooms themselves. Take the La-Z-Boy, for instance: after its recliners rose to prominence with television culture during the 1960s, La-Z-Boy introduced chairs with compartments for storing snacks and remote controls in the 1980s.[1] In 2000, Earl and Paula Wiley patented the first armchair with a built-in universal remote control, an armchair that also *was* a remote control.[2] As I mentioned in Chapter 3, widescreen and HD television sets would never have developed without remote control, and big-screen TVs fed the popularity of open-concept living rooms in the United States. Frank Lloyd Wright, the architect behind the first entertainment room, was also instrumental in bringing open-concept architecture to private homes. This design principle reached its popular apex in the late twentieth and early twenty-first centuries with the help of electronics that could be enjoyed and controlled at a distance. Imagine the frustration of trying to watch a twenty-inch television in a 500-square-foot living room. No one would design a house so poorly suited to its occupants' lifestyle. But with a big-screen TV, parents can have a glass of wine in their open-concept kitchen while keeping an eye on what their kids are watching in the living room. Remote controls also help because they mitigate the hassle of moving across these giant rooms every time you want to change a channel or adjust the volume.

People may be living things, but we are things all the same. We too can be changed by objects in our environments, including remote controls. Remote controls encourage us to spend more time sitting down. They may make us sedentary, slow down our metabolisms, and increase our body-fat percentages. They may also affect what we experience and believe the media to be. Design theorists claim that "material artifacts configure (rather than simply meet) what consumers and users experience as needs and desires."[3] Put simply: remote controls are changing not only our bodies but also our minds. They were designed to help us avoid radio and television commercials, but they also make such interruptions more annoying. While holding a remote, I expect to be able to skip advertisements but that's not an expectation I can always realize. Some video-on-demand providers now disable the fast-forward command during playback, for instance. Broadcasters have gotten savvier about varying the frequency and duration of commercial interruptions in order to keep viewers tuned into their programs, and advertisers have also developed new narrative and aesthetic strategies to increase viewers' interest in their commercials. In short, what the media is and how it operates have been shaped by remote control. "The media" doesn't only include movies, television shows, and news reports. We cannot just think about this content outside its material context, because our experiences of sounds and images are deeply informed by the material objects that deliver them.

The remote control is only one such object. While my living room contains four remotes, it also holds over a dozen DVD box sets of classic (and kitsch) television shows as well as an abundance of devices for playing video games, including an Xbox 360, laptop, iPad, and iPhone. These objects could all inspire significant questions about how material culture is shaping twenty-first-century media practices. How does the packaging of DVD box sets contribute to the practice of binge watching and our ambivalent characterization of it as both connoisseurship and procrastination? How does the current variety of video game platforms affect our understanding of what a video game is? Does playing the same game with an iPhone touch screen, a computer keyboard, and an

Xbox controller change my experience of suspense or my investment in my character's goals? This book cannot answer these questions, but I hope it helps you ask more like them. Media is something we touch as well as something we watch, and we need to take its objects seriously—to ask where they came from, who made them, and what cultural values they reflect—if we want to understand ourselves and our world.

# NOTES

## Introduction

1 "remote control, *n.*", OED Online (June 2014), Oxford University Press. http://www.oed.com.proxy.library. georgetown.edu/view/Entry/241703?isAdvanced=false& result=1&rskey=XQ4Gq5& (accessed June 26, 2014).

2 John Barrell and John Mee (eds), *Trials for Treason and Sedition, 1792–1974*, vol. 5 (London: Pickering and Chatto, 2006), 201; emphasis mine.

3 "remote control, *n.*", OED Online.

4 Nikola Tesla, "Method of and Apparatus for Controlling Mechanism of Moving Vessels or Vehicles," US Patent 613,809, filed July 1, 1898 and issued November 8, 1898, in Nikola Tesla, *The Complete Patents of Nikola Tesla*, edited by Jim Glenn (New York: Barnes and Noble, 1994), 318.

5 Marc J. Seifer, *Wizard: The Life and Times of Nikola Tesla: Biography of a Genius* (Secaucus, NJ: Carol, 1996), 195.

6 P. W. Singer, *Wired for War: The Robotics Revolution and Conflict in the Twenty-First Century* (New York: Penguin), 46–7.

7 Seifer, *Wizard*, 196; Singer, *Wired for War*, 46–7.

8 Walter V. Ash, "Apparatus for Remote Control of Electric Motors," US Patent 738,893, filed January 2, 1903 and issued September 8, 1903. https://www.google.com/patents/US738393?dq=%22remote + control%22&hl=en&sa=X&ei=NaC9U6LNCI-ZyAT51YG4BQ&ved=0CFoQ6AEwCTgy (accessed July 10, 2014).

9 Jeffrey Sconce, *Haunted Media: Electronic Presence from Telegraphy to Television* (Durham, NC: Duke University Press, 2000), 21–91.

10 C. Baber and N. A. Stanton, "Defining 'Problem Spaces' in VCR Use: The Application of Task Analysis for Error Identification," in *Contemporary Ergonomics: Ergonomics for Industry*, edited by E. J. Lovejoy (Cleveland, OH: CRC Press, 1992), 418–23.

11 Steven Jones, "Controllers," in *Debugging Game History*, edited by Raiford Guins and Henry Lowood (Cambridge, MA: MIT Press, forthcoming).

# Chapter 1

1 "New Radio Control," *Montreal Gazette*, June 20, 1929, 147.

2 "New Radio Control."

3 "New Radio Control."

4 Jeff Nilsson, "Losing Touch: The Evolution of Remote Controls," *Saturday Evening Post*, June 9, 2010. http://www.saturdayeveningpost.com/2012/06/09/archives/post-perspective/evolution-remote-controls.html (accessed July 10, 2014).

5 Tom Volek, "Searching for the Social Construction of Radio," *American Journalism* 9, 3–4 (June 1992): 46.

**6** Lynn Spigel, *Make Room for TV: Television and the Family Ideal in Postwar America* (Chicago: University of Chicago Press, 1992), 12–13.

**7** Elizabeth Faue, "Electricity, 1900–1930," in *Encyclopedia of American History: The Emergence of Modern America, 1900 to 1928*, vol. VII, edited by Elizabeth Faue and Gary B. Nash, revised edn (New York: Facts On File, Inc., 2010), 82–3.

**8** Spigel, *Make Room for TV*, 21.

**9** Joan DeJean, "Who Lives in this Room?," *New York Times*, July 19, 2010. http://opinionator.blogs.nytimes.com/2010/07/19/who-lives-in-this-room/?_php=true&_type=blogs&_r=0 (accessed July 10, 2014).

**10** Christine Frederick, "Home Comforts," *Wireless Age* (January 1925): 36–8, 83, 85–6, quoted in Richard Butsch, *The Making of American Audiences: From Stage to Television, 1750–1990* (New York: Cambridge University Press), 193.

**11** *Ladies' Home Journal* (December 1925), 179, quoted in Louis Carlat, "A Cleanser for the Mind: Marketing Radio Receivers for the American Home, 1922–1932," in *His and Hers: Gender, Consumption, and Technology*, edited by Roger Horowitz and Arwen Mohun (Charlottesville: University of Virginia Press, 1998), 129.

**12** J. D. Relyea, "Tuning the Radio From Your Arm Chair," *The Canadian Magazine* 73 (February 1930): 40.

**13** Spigel, *Make Room for TV*, 29.

**14** Journal unknown (1932), 104. I purchased a number of the ads described in this book through online auctions. Consequently, full publication information was not always available. I provide it to the best of my ability.

**15** *Ladies' Home Journal* (March 1933), 131.

**16**  *Collier's* (December 1, 1933), 6.

**17**  Journal unknown (December 19, 1931), 43.

**18**  Relyea, "Tuning the Radio from Your Arm Chair," 40.

**19**  "New Methods Make Remote Controls Popular," *Popular Science Monthly* 124 (January 1934): 54.

**20**  Volek, "Searching for the Social Construction of Radio," 48.

**21**  David Sarnoff, "Radio Music Box," in *Music, Sound, and Technology in America: A Documentary History of Early Phonograph, Cinema, and Radio*, edited by Timothy D. Taylor, Mark Katz, and Tony Grajeda (Durham, NC: Duke University Press, 2012), 260.

**22**  Other countries employed different funding models; the British Broadcasting Company, for instance, reduced commercial messages through license fees attached to radio receiver sales.

**23**  "Radio Broadcast Advertisements; Airphone Advertising Will Kill Fan Interest," in *Music, Sound, and Technology in America: A Documentary History of Early Phonograph, Cinema, and Radio*, edited by Timothy D. Taylor, Mark Katz, and Tony Grajeda (Durham, NC: Duke University Press, 2012), 289.

**24**  Hanno Hardt, *In the Company of Media: Cultural Constructions of Communication 1920's–1930's* (Boulder, CO: Westview Press, 1999), 131.

**25**  Hardt, *In the Company of Media*, 132.

**26**  Inger L. Stole, *Advertising on Trial: Consumer Activism and Corporate Public Relations in the 1930s* (Champaign: University of Illinois Press, 2006), 30.

**27**  Relyea, "Tuning the Radio from Your Arm Chair," 40.

**28** Alfred P. Lane, "Radio Aims at Remote Control," *Popular Science Monthly* (November 1930), 78.

**29** *Saturday Evening Post* (October 1, 1938), 3.

**30** *Philco Serviceman* (October 1938), Philco Radio & Television Corporation, quoted in "Mystery Control History: How It All Came About," *Philco Repair Bench*. http://www.philcorepair bench.com/mystery/history.htm (accessed July 10, 2014).

**31** Patrick Parsons, "The 'Most Thrilling Invention Since Radio Itself': The Evolution of the Radio Remote Control in the 1920s and 1930s," *Journal of Radio & Audio Media* 21, 1 (2014): 75.

**32** "Postwar American Television: Early Remote Controls," *The Early Television Museum*. http://www.earlytelevision.org/ remotes.html (accessed July 10, 2014).

**33** Wayne C. Luplow and John I. Taylor, "Channel Surfing Redux," *IEEE Consumer Electronics Magazine* 1, 4 (October 2012): 9.

**34** *Newsweek* (month unknown, 1951), 57.

**35** Publication information unknown; featured in "Television: TV in the Antenna Age," San Francisco International Airport Museum, San Francisco International Airport, Terminal 3, F2 North Connect Gallery, August 2011 through February 2012.

**36** Spigel, *Make Room for TV*, 128–9.

**37** Lynn Spigel, "Installing the Television Set: Popular Discourse on Television and Domestic Space," *Camera Obscura* 16, 1 (Winter 1988): 13–14; and Spigel, *Make Room for TV*, 128–9.

**38** Laura Alpern, "The Story of Blab-Off," *The Early Television Museum*. http://www.earlytelevision.org/blab_off.html (accessed July 10, 2014).

**39** Alpern, "The Story of Blab-Off."

**40** C. L. Walker, "How to Stop Objectionable TV Commercials," *Reader's Digest*, November 1953, 72.

**41** Walker, "How to Stop Objectionable TV Commercials," 71–2.

# Chapter 2

**1** Ken Auletta, "CBS, Time Warner Cable, and the Disruption of TV," *The New Yorker*, August 19, 2013. http://www.newyorker.com/business/currency/cbs-time-warner-cable-and-the-disruption-of-tv (accessed July 10, 2014).

**2** George V. Higgins, "Television: Much of a Muchness," *Wall Street Journal*, November 10, 1986, 1.

**3** As communications historian Bruce C. Klopfenstein notes, because remote controls are mostly sold as accessories and do not have their own Standard Industry Classification code, there is little reliable data on remote control sales or household integration. Nevertheless, he cites 1986 as the year when color television sales, VCR sales, and cable box rentals *probably* pushed remote control penetration past 50 percent. Bruce C. Klopfenstein, "From Gadget to Necessity: The Diffusion of Remote Control Technology," in *The Remote Control in the New Age of Television*, edited by James R. Walker and Robert V. Bellamy, Jr. (Westport, CT: Praeger, 1993), 32.

**4** *Saturday Evening Post* (September 10, 1955), 146–7.

**5** *Saturday Evening Post* (September 10, 1955), 146–7.

**6** Paul F. Lazarsfeld and Robert K. Merton, "Mass Communication, Popular Taste, and Organized Social Action," in

*Media Studies: A Reader*, edited by Paul Marris, Caroline Bassett, and Sue Thornham, 2nd ed. (New York: New York University Press, 2000), 22–3.

7   Spigel, *Make Room for TV*, 60–5.

8   Klopfenstein, "From Gadget to Necessity," 24.

9   Bob Baker, "Revolution By Remote," *Los Angeles Times*, April 13, 2003. http://www.articles.latimes.com/2003/apr/13/ entertainment/ca-baker13 (accessed July 10, 2014); Alexander J. Field, "Table Dg117-130: Radio and television – stations, sets produced, and households with sets: 1921–2000," in *Historical Statistics of the United States, Earliest Times to the Present: Millennial Edition*, vol. IV, edited by Susan B. Carter, Scott Sigmund Gartner, Michael R. Haines, Alan L. Olmstead, Richard Sutch, and Gavin Wright (New York: Cambridge University Press, 2006), 1027–8.

10   William Feingold, "Ultrasonic TV Remote Controls," *Electronics World* 64, 2 (August 1960): 54.

11   *The News from Frederick, Maryland*, March 15, 1961, 11. http://www.newspapers.com/newspage/7934680/ (accessed July 10, 2014).

12   "Admiral Loses Suit on Zenith Patents," *New York Times 1923–Current File*, September 1, 1960. http://search.proquest. com/docview/115163742?accountid=1109 (accessed July 10, 2014).

13   *Zenith Radio Corp. v. Admiral Corporation* 190 F. SUPP. 41 (W.D. OKLA. 1960). https://www.casetext.com/case/zenith-radio-corporation-v-admiral-corporation#.U68CU41dWpd (accessed July 10, 2014).

14   "TV Sets with Remote Control," *Consumer Reports* (March 24, 1959), 113.

**15** Klopfenstein, "From Gadget to Necessity," 25. For a survey of remote control narratives in literature and television, see Jan Holmberg, "Remote Control: Contextualizing a Modern Device," in *Screen Culture: History and Textuality*, edited by J. Fullerton (Bloomington, IN: John Libbey, 2004), 221–7; David Freedman, "Remote Remake," *Ironic Sans*, May 29, 2006. http://www.ironicsans.com/2006/05/remote_remake.html (accessed July 10, 2014); and Jeff Thoss, "'Some Weird Kind of Video Feedback Time Warp Zapping Thing': Television, Remote Controls, and Metalepsis," in *Metalepsis in Popular Culture*, edited by Karin Kukkonen and Sonja Klimek (New York: De Gruyter, 2011), 158–70.

**16** Origin and date unknown.

**17** Lisa Parks, "Cracking Open the Set: Television Repair and Tinkering with Gender, 1949–1955," *Television New Media* 1, 3 (August 2000): 257–78; Max Dawson, "'Look out, Gracie': Gendering the Television Remote Control," *Television Futures*, July 24, 2012. http://www.televisionfutures.wordpress.com/tag/zenith/ (accessed July 10, 2014); and Spigel, *Make Room for TV*.

**18** Bill Osgerby, "The Bachelor Pad as Cultural Icon: Masculinity, Consumption and Interior Design in American Men's Magazines," *Journal of Design History* 18, 1 (Spring 2005): 110.

**19** Electronics repair and technological connoisseurship also fueled a contemporaneous gendered interest in hi-fi stereo electronics; see Keir Keightley, "'Turn it Down!' She Shrieked: Gender, Domestic Space, and High Fidelity," *Popular Music* 15, 2 (May 1996): 150, 156–9.

**20** Parks, "Cracking Open the Set," 262.

**21** One *Financial Times* article cites a gender-reversed version of this ad in which Allen mutes Burns. Evidence suggests that Zenith ran that ad far less often than the one described here. I have also been unable to locate a physical copy of the ad itself. Joe Moran, "Defining Moment: Zenith Perfects the TV Remote Control, 1956," *Financial Times Magazine*, May 1, 2010. http://www.ft.com/cms/s/2/03919ef2-51a2-11df-bed9-00144feab49a.html#axzz357SSDpWx (accessed June 14, 2014).

22  "TV Ad—RCA Victor Wireless Wizard Remote Control 1960s with Vaughn Monroe," MyFootage.Com. http://www.myfootage.com/details.php?gid=58&sgid=&pid=20592 (accessed July 10, 2014); "TV Sets with Remote Control," 113.

23  Karal Ann Marling, *As Seen On TV: The Visual Culture of Everyday Life in the 1950s* (Cambridge, MA: Harvard University Press, 1996), 188. To this day, the Eisenhower National Historic Site continues to assure young visitors that President and Mrs. Eisenhower preferred television tray tables to their White House dining room; "Eisenhower Virtual Home Tour," *Eisenhower National Historic Site*, National Parks Service. http://www.nps.gov/features/eise/jrranger/tour4xxA.htm (accessed July 10, 2014).

24  Marling, *As Seen On TV*, 191–2.

25  Marling, *As Seen On TV*, 190–1.

26  Marling, *As Seen On TV*, 235.

27  Marling, *As Seen On TV*, 236.

28  Klopfenstein, "From Gadget to Necessity," 25.

29  RCA Victor, "Television Remote Control (Tuner) (ca. 1961)," Prelinger Archives Online, Library of Congress. https://www.archive.org/details/Televisi1961 (accessed July 10, 2014).

30  Brian Winston, "How Are Media Born?," in *Media Studies: A Reader*, edited by Paul Marris, Caroline Bassett, and Sue

Thornham, 2nd edn (New York: New York University Press, 2000), 797.

31 Patrick R. Parsons, *Blue Skies: A History of Cable Television* (Philadelphia: Temple University Press, 2008), 436–7.

32 In 1950, only 14,000 US households subscribed to CATV. There were still only 650,000 CATV subscribers in 1960, a very small number compared to the over fifty million subscribers receiving cable today (with another forty-four million paying for television content via satellite or other telecommunications service). CATV was a solution for broadcast problems; it was not an alternative to broadcast television. "Evolution of Cable," *Federal Communications Commission*. http://www.fcc.gov/encyclopedia/evolution-cable-television (accessed July 10, 2014); see also Megan Mullen, *The Rise of Cable Programming in the United States: Revolution or Evolution?* (Austin: University of Texas Press, 2003).

33 Mullen, *The Rise of Cable Programming in the United States*, 104–9.

34 Mullen, *The Rise of Cable Programming in the United States*, 96.

35 "Cable's Story," National Cable and Telecommunications Association. http://www.ncta.com/who-we-are/our-story (accessed July 10, 2014).

36 Klopfenstein, "From Gadget to Necessity," 28–9.

37 In the 1970s, cable providers transmitted their programming via very high frequency (VHF) and later ultra-high frequency (UHF) radio waves passed through coaxial cables. There are only twelve designated VHF channels—hence the twelve buttons for twelve stations on the first Jerrold cable converter remotes. Later on, providers developed a technique known as frequency division multiplexing to transmit more stations over

the same bandwidth, which is why 1990s cable subscribers could receive up to five hundred stations on the same analog coaxial cables.

**38**  Some critics argue that VHS beat Betamax because its tapes were quicker to dub, which led to early support from the pornography industry. Others suggest that VHS's four-hour cassettes made the format more popular with viewers because they could hold entire football games on a single tape. For more on the VHS–Betamax format wars, see Frederick Wasser, *Veni, Vidi, Video: The Hollywood Empire and the VCR* (Austin: University of Texas Press, 2002); and James Lardner, *Fast Forward: Hollywood, the Japanese, and the Onslaught of the VCR* (New York: Norton, 1987).

**39**  Journal unknown (December 1980), page number unknown.

**40**  E. Fred Schubert, *Light-Emitting Diodes* (New York: Cambridge University Press, 2003), 6, 8.

**41**  Jeffrey Bausch, "The Long History of Light-Emitting Diodes," *Electronic Products*, August 31, 2011. http://www.electronicproducts.com/Optoelectronics/LEDs/The_long_history_of_light-emitting_diodes.aspx (accessed July 10, 2014).

**42**  Klopfenstein, "From Gadget to Necessity," 33.

**43**  "Logitech Study Shows Multiple Remote Controls Hindering Entertainment Experiences Around the Globe."

**44**  Patrick M. Reilly, "High-Tech Clutter Haunts the Home." *The Globe and Mail*, January 11, 1997, C21.

**45**  Lynn Spigel (ed.), "The Suburban Home Companion: Television and the Neighborhood Ideal in Postwar America," in *Welcome to the Dreamhouse: Popular Media and the Postwar Suburbs* (Durham, NC: Duke University Press, 2001), 40.

**46** Sam Biddle, "The IKEA TV Reviewed," *Gizmodo*, June 18, 2012. http://www.gizmodo.com/5919216/the-ikea-tv-worse-than-assembling-100-bookshelves-at-once (accessed July 10, 2014).

**47** Klopfenstein, "From Gadget to Necessity," 32–3.

**48** Jeff Menne, email to author, August 2, 2014.

**49** "Logitech Study Shows Multiple Remote Controls Hindering Entertainment Experiences Around the Globe."

# Chapter 3

**1** Klopfenstein, "From Gadget to Necessity," 33.

**2** Tom Shales, "Television's Shattering Decade," *Washington Post*, December 31, 1991. http://www.lexisnexis.com/hottopics/lnacademic (accessed July 29, 2014).

**3** The Japanese manufacturer TOTO introduced a remote control bidet, the Washlet, in 1996. James Barron, "Will the User Snap Before the Lid Does?" *New York Times*, March 28, 1996. http://www.nytimes.com/1996/03/28/garden/will-the-user-snap-before-the-lid-does.html (accessed July 29, 2014).

**4** Anthony Ramirez, "When the New Remotes Zap, Everything Listens," *New York Times*, June 24, 1993. http://www.nytimes.com/1993/06/24/news/field-test-when-the-new-remotes-zap-everything-listens.html (accessed July 29, 2014).

**5** Jennifer Lee, "The Ultimate Remote Means Never Having to Leave the Couch," *New York Times*, September 14, 2000. http://www.nytimes.com/2000/09/14/technology/14REMO.html (accessed July 29, 2014).

**6** Ivan Berger, "Coping with Remote-Control Clutter," *New York Times*, May 13, 1989. http://www.nytimes.com/1989/05/13/

style/consumer-s-world-coping-with-remote-control-clutter.
html (accessed July 29, 2014).

**7**  Ivan Berger, "Coping with Electronic Clutter At Home,"
*New York Times*, February 16, 1991. http://www.nytimes.
com/1991/02/16/news/coping-with-electronic-clutter-at-
home.html (accessed July 29, 2014); Lori Baird, *Cut the
Clutter and Stow the Stuff: The Q.U.I.C.K. Way to Bring Lasting
Order to Household Chaos* (Emmaus, PA: Rodale Books,
2002), 126.

**8**  Hans Fantel, "Simplified Home Systems," *New York Times*,
September 21, 1986. http://www.nytimes.com/1986/09/21/
magazine/simplified-home-systems.html (accessed July
29, 2014); Robert Adler, quoted in Vic Sussman, "Remote
Possibilities," *Washington Post Magazine*, March 8,
1987, W67.

**9**  Casey Johnston, "Smart TVs Have A Serious Communication
Problem," *Ars Technica*, February 20, 2013. http://
arstechnica.com/gadgets/2013/02/smart-tvs-have-a-serious-
communication-problem/ (accessed July 29, 2014).

**10**  Barry Meier, "VCRs Have Too Many Buttons? Here's Help
(Note the Buttons)," *New York Times*, December 28, 1991.
http://www.nytimes.com/1991/12/28/news/vcr-have-too-
many-buttons-here-s-help-note-the-buttons.html (accessed
July 29, 2014).

**11**  Edward Rothstein, "Remotes: On Fast Forward," *New
York Times*, October 11, 1990. http://www.nytimes.
com/1990/10/11/garden/electronics-notebook-remotes-on-
fast-forward.html (accessed July 29, 2014).

**12**  Henry Jenkins, *Convergence Culture: Where Old and New
Media Collide* (New York: New York University Press,
2008), 14.

**13** Hans Fantel, "Home Video: The World At One's Fingertips," *New York Times*, December 1, 1985. http://www.nytimes.com/1985/12/01/arts/home-video-the-world-at-one-s-fingertips.html (accessed July 29, 2014).

**14** Berger, "Coping with Remote-Control Clutter."

**15** Hans Fantel, "Remote-Control Units: Getting to Know Them," *New York Times*, March 6, 1986. http://www.nytimes.com/1986/03/06/garden/remote-control-units-getting-to-know-them.html (accessed July 29, 2014).

**16** *Popular Science* (December 1984), page number unknown.

**17** Handy (Jam) Organization, "Television Remote Control (Tuner)," RCA Victor. https://www.archive.org/details/Televisi1961 (accessed July 21, 2014).

**18** Journal, date, and page number unknown.

**19** Journal unknown, 1986, page number unknown.

**20** Fantel, "Home Video: The World at One's Fingertips"; Hans Fantel, "Tuning Fine Systems," *New York Times*, September 22, 1985. http://www.nytimes.com/1990/04/22/magazine/fine-tuning.html (accessed July 29, 2014).

**21** Fantel, "Tuning Fine Systems."

**22** Barbara Klinger, *Beyond the Multiplex: Cinema, New Technologies, and the Home* (Berkeley: University of California Press, 2006), 17.

**23** Spigel, *Make Room for TV*, 181–7.

**24** Fantel, "Home Video: The World at One's Fingertips"; Fantel, "Tuning Fine Systems."

**25** Klinger, *Beyond the Multiplex*, 18.

**26** Klinger, *Beyond the Multiplex*, 20.

**27** CL9, *CORE Reference Manual* (1987), v.

**28**  There are enough minor differences in the autopairing procedures of various preprogrammed universal remote controls to render a more accurate summary of the process pointless. If you want to learn how to program your personal universal remote, I recommend searching for its particular manufacturer and model number online.

**29**  Baber and Stanton, "Defining 'Problem Spaces' in VCR Use: The Application of Task Analysis for Error Identification."

**30**  May Wong, "Proliferation of Remotes Turns Off Consumers," *Los Angeles Times*, July 6, 2004. http://articles.latimes.com/2004/jul/06/business/fi-remote6 (accessed July 29, 2014).

**31**  Wong, "Proliferation of Remotes Turns Off Consumers."

**32**  For more on the conflict between product-centered and user-centered design, see Elizabeth Shove, Matthew Watson, Martin Hand, and Jack Ingram, *The Design of Everyday Life* (New York: Berg, 2007), 125–34.

**33**  Donald R. Gentner and Jonathan Grudin, "Why Good Engineers (Sometimes) Create Bad Interfaces," *CHI '90 Proceedings*, April 1990, 277.

**34**  Rothstein, "Remotes: On Fast Forward."

**35**  Fantel, "Remote-Control Units: Getting To Know Them."

**36**  Dean Takahashi, "New Remote Control Unit Is a 'Design Marvel,'" *Los Angeles Times*, October 15, 1990. http://articles.latimes.com/1990-10-05/business/fi-1774_1_remote-control (accessed July 29, 2014).

**37**  Peter Edward Lowe, quoted in Takahashi, "New Remote Control Unit Is a 'Design Marvel.'"

**38**  Ramirez, "When New Remotes Zap, Everything Listens."

**39**  "What a Joy to Hold," *Business Week*, June 6, 1993. http://www.businessweek.com/stories/1993-06-06/what-a-joy-to-hold

(accessed July 29, 2014); "Fetish Toys for the Truly Wired." *Wired* 1, 4 (September/October 1993). http://archive.wired.com/wired/archive/1.04/fetish.html (accessed July 29, 2014).

**40** Kathleen Kerwin, "The Double Deck Woes of Go-Video," *Business Week*, July 1, 1991. http://www.businessweek.com/stories/1991-06-30/the-double-deck-woes-of-go-video (accessed July 29, 2014).

**41** Katie Hafner, "Now Preening on a Coffee Table," *New York Times*, February 19, 2004. http://www.nytimes.com/2004/02/19/technology/now-preening-on-the-coffee-table.html (accessed July 29, 2014).

**42** "What a Joy to Hold."

**43** Paul Newby, quoted in Christopher Mascari, "Story of a Peanut," *Gizmodo*, June 20, 2008. http://www.gizmodo.com/5017972/story-of-a-peanut-the-tivo-remotes-untold-past-present-and-future (accessed July 29, 2014); Paul Newby, quoted in William Lidwell and Gerry Manacsa, *Deconstructing Product Design: Exploring the Form, Function, Usability, Sustainability, and Commercial Success of 100 Amazing Products* (Minneapolis: Rockport Publishers, 2011), 158.

**44** Phone conversation with Doug Patton, May 6, 2014.

**45** Kara Swisher, "Your Show of Shows," *Washington Post*, February 16, 1996, B01.

**46** "TV Times," *Design Week*, February 12, 1998. http://www.designweek.co.uk/news/tv-times/1132132.article (accessed July 29, 2014).

**47** "Interaction Packed," *Design Week*, April 23, 1998. http://www.designweek.co.uk/news/interaction-packed/1115353.article (accessed July 29, 2014).

# Afterword

**1** Michael Hauser, email to author, September 18, 2014. For more on the history of recliners and television culture, see Cecelia Tichi, *Electronic Hearth: Creating an American Television Culture* (New York: Oxford University Press, 1992), 84–103.

**2** Earl Jansen Wiley, Universal Remote Control Chair, US Patent 20120280544, filed May 6, 2011, and issued November 8, 2012. http://www.google.com/patents/US20120280544 (accessed July 28, 2014).

**3** Shove et al., *The Design of Everyday Life*, 134.

# INDEX

Note: Page references for illustrations appear in *italics*.

Access   97
Adler, Robert   89, 106
Admiral Corporation
    56–8, *57*
    Son-R   56–8, *57*
advertising *see* commercials
Air Egg *see* RM-VP1 Remote
    Commander
Ali, Mohammed   73
Allen, Gracie   64, *65*
Alpern, Laura   40
amateur radio   5–6, *7*
American Dream   18
*American Home*   82
Apple   xi, 91, 92, 119, 120–3,
    *121,* 128
    Apple I   101
    Apple II   101
    Apple Remote   92, 119,
       120–3, *121*
    Apple TV   xi, 92, 120–3
    iPad   121, 128

iPhone   121, 128
iPod   120, 121
Apple I   101
Apple II   101
Apple Remote   92, 119,
    120–3, *121*
Apple TV   xi, 92, 120–3
Aristotle   8
Armour   69
*Ars Technica*   89
Ash, Walter V.   xv
aspirational norms   44–5, 46,
    59, 69–70, 85–6, 88
AT&T   73
Atwater Kent   10
AV500   97

Bang & Olufsen   99–100
    Beo5000   99–100
Beo5000   99–100
Berger, Ivan   88, 89
Betamax   76–8, *78*

*Beyond the Multiplex: Cinema, New Technologies, and the Home* (Klinger) 98–9
Blab-Off 39–41, 58
black box 92, 120–3
Boas, Franz 125
Burns, George 64, *65*
*Business Week* 109

cable boxes 4, 81, 98
cable broadcasting 41, 47, 71–6, 81, 84, 117–18
Cal-Dak 67
*Canadian Magazine* 11
CATV *see* Community Antenna Television (CATV)
channel surfing xix, 41, 43–4, 46, 72, 114–16, 118, 126
Christian Broadcast Network 73
CL9 CORE 101–3, *102,* 105, 106–7
*Clara, Lu and Em* 26
Colgate-Palmolive 26
Colortrak 2000 95
Columaire 21–2
commercials xvii, 3, 5, 11, 23–5, 26, 33–5, 39–41, 45, 49, 60, 62, 66, 73, 77, 86, 127–8

Community Antenna Television (CATV) 72–3
computers 4, 74, 99–105, 112, 120–1, 128
Conrac 39
    Fleetwood 39
conspicuous consumption 13–16, 61
Consumer Electronics Association 115
*Consumer Reports* 58–9
control
    American Dream 18
    applications 121–2
    aspirational norm 44–5, 46, 59, 69–70, 85–6, 88
    black box 92, 120–3
    branded xix, 86, 90, 92, 93–100, 105–13, 112
    cable broadcasting 41, 47, 71–6, 81, 84, 117–18
    celebrity endorsement 64–6, *65*
    channel surfing xix, 41, 43–4, 46, 72, 114–16, 118, 126
    clutter xix, 46, 82–3, 85, 88, 89, 91, 93–4, 97
    cohabitation 93
    commercials xvii, 3, 5, 11, 23–5, 26, 33, 34–5, 39–41, 45, 49, 60, 62, 66, 73, 77, 86, 127–8

computers 100–5
confusion xix–xx
consumption xii, xix, 3,
13–14, 17, 18–19, 21, 25,
30, 41–2, 61, 67–9, 72, 82,
86, 92, 94, 98, 107–8, 126
corporate loyalty 96
cultural artifacts xiii
democracy xiii–xiv
design xiv, xvii–xviii, xx,
1, *2,* 3, 4, 5, 14–18, *15,*
*17,* 20, 22, 27, 30, 33,
39, 47–56, *48, 50–1, 55,*
*57,* 66, 70–7, *71, 75, 78,*
79–81, 88, 89–91, *91,*
93–117, *95, 102, 109,*
*110, 115,* 120–3, *121,*
124, 125–8
domesticity 22–3, 38, 41,
44, 45–6, 48, 66–9, 76,
77, 82–4, 96, 99, 126, 127
empowerment xii, xiv,
xvii–xviii, xix, 5, 46,
86, 92
engagement xix, 46, 49,
66, 69
entertainment centers 56,
82–4, 96, 98, 99
ergonomics 113–16
family dynamic 28–9, 35,
37–8, 41, 64, 86, 126, 127
fast-forward xiii, xiv, 77,
114, 116, 122, 128

freedom 41, 46, 78, 85
future 123–4
gender roles xiii, 20, 21,
26, 35, 36, 37, 47, 49, *50,*
52, 60–2, 64, 126
history xiv–xvi, 1–4, 5–24
home theater 98–100, 112
ideology xvi–xvii
inconvenience 88–91,
101–5, 107–8, 111, 112,
118–19, 124
interaction xii, 118
leisure xii, 9–10, 60, 62
luxury xii, 4, 5, 16, 18, 23,
45, 62, 79, 86, 92, 97
marketing xii, xvii, 3–4,
5, 13–14, 16–17, 18, 20,
21, 23–4, 34–7, *36,*
40–1, 45–6, 47, 49, 52,
58, 59–62, 64–6, *65,* 70,
77, 87–8, 90, 94, 96–7,
107–8, 111
mass media 4, 23, 49, 124,
126, 128–9
middle class 4, 5, 7, 13, 17,
18, 21, 33
military xv
mute xvii, 41, 53, 54
passivity 58–9, 66, 68, 76,
79, 118
patents xv–xvi, 56, 58, *110*
pause 77
programming 100–5

promise 97–8
radio xii, xiv, xv, xvi, xviii, 1–4, *2,* 5–32, 47
reliability 58–9
remoteness xvi–xvii
rewind 77
routine 4
social advancement xii, 13–14, 21, 44–5, 99
sophistication xii, 4
sovereignty xii, xiv, xix, 85, 96, 99
technology xii, xv–xvi, 4–5, 20, 22, 29, 33, 39, 45–6, 47–56, 60, 61–2, 65–6, 70–7, 79–81, 87, 89–91, 93–113, 120–9
television xi, xii, xviii, 32–42, 44–86, 87–124
universal xix, 86, 90, 100–13, *115,* 119
video games xviii, 83, 84, 101, 116, 117, 128
controllers xviii, 116–18
cowboys 61–2
Cox Cable 117
see also cable broadcasting

d'Aviler, Charles 9
Dawson, Max 60
*Design Week* 118, 119
Digital Command Center 94–5, *95,* 96–7, 100

digital video disc (DVD) see DVD
digital video recorder (DVR) see DVR
Dimensia Digital Control 94–7, *95,* 101, 114
direction pad see D-pad
DIRECTV xi
D-pad 116–19, 122
Dupont 69
Durkheim, Émile 125
DVD 87, 104, 119, 128
DVR 113–17

Eisenhower, Dwight D. 67
Eisenhower Interstate Act 38
1898 Electrical Exhibition xiv, xv
Electric Wonderbar 67
electronic program guides (EPGs) 43, 117–18, 119
Electronics Industry Association 88
*Electronics World* 54
Emerson 39
EPGs see electronic program guides (EPGs)
ESPN 73

Fantel, Hans 89, 93, 97, 107
fast-forward xiii, xiv, 77, 114, 116, 122, 128

FCC *see* Federal
        Communications
        Commission (FCC)
Federal Communications
        Commission
        (FCC)   74
*fernlenkboote see* FL-7
FL-7 xv
Flash-Matic   41, 47–56, *48,*
        *50–1,* 79, 113
Fleetwood   39
Foresight 70   97
Frazier, Joe   73
Frederick, Christine   10
French Revolution   xiii

Gabet, André   xv
Garod   32–3, 41
        Telezoom   32–3, 41
General Electric   39
General Motors Radio
        Company   14–16, *15,*
        23, 281
        remote   14–16, *15,* 23
Gentner, Donald R.   106
*George Burns and Gracie Allen*
        *Show*   64, *65*
Google TV   118
Go-Video   109–11, *110,* 112
        Palm-Mate   109–10, *110,*
        111, 112, 113
        VCR-2   110–11
Grudin, Jonathan   106

Hamlin Electronics   75
ham radio *see* amateur radio
Hardy, Thomas   xiii–xiv
HBO   73
hobbyists *see* amateur radio
Hoffman   58
Hollyhock House (Wright)   82
Home Box Office (HBO)
        *see* HBO
home theater   98–100, 112
home video   47, 76, 87, 119

IKEA   84
        Uppleva   84
Industrial Design Excellence
        Awards   108
infrared LEDs   79–81, 84, 87
Intellivision   117
iPad   121, 128
iPhone   121, 128
iPod   120, 121

Jenkins, Henry   91–2
Jerrold   74–5, *75*
Johnston, Casey   89

K-45   1–4, *2,* 12, 14, 16
Kinect   123
Klinger, Barbara   98
        *Beyond the Multiplex:*
        *Cinema, New*
        *Technologies, and the*
        *Home*   98–9

Kolster   1–4, *2*, 12, 14, 16
    K-45   1–4, *2*, 12, 14, 16

*Ladies' Home Journal*   10, 60
Lane, Alfred P.   27–9, *28*
    Radio Aims at Remote
        Control   27–9, *28*
Laserdisc   88, 116, 119
La-Z-Boy   126
Lazy Bones   33–9, *36*, 41,
    64, 113
Lazy-X   16–18, *17*
LEDs *see* infrared LEDs
light-emitting diodes (LEDs)
    *see* infrared LEDs
*Los Angeles Times*   106

McDonald, Eugene F. Jr
    34, 41
Magic Brain   39
Manischewitz, Howard   39–41
    Blab-Off   39–41, 58
March, H. Colley   122
Marconi, Guglielmo   xv
Marling, Karal Ann   66, 68
mass media   4, 23, 49, 124,
    126, 128–9
Mattel   117
    Intellivision   117
Medalist   39
Milford, Sir John   xiii–xiv
Mitsubishi   108, *109*
    PRM-1   108, *109*

Monroe, Vaughn   65–6
Morgan, Lewis Henry   125
MOS 6052   101
Motorola   58
MSN TV   118
Museum of Modern Art   109
    Mutant Materials in
        Contemporary
        Design   109
Mutant Materials in
    Contemporary
    Design   109
mute   xvii, 41, 53, 54
Mystery Control   29–30, *31*

National Broadcasting
    Company (NBC)   7
NBC *see* National Broadcasting
    Company (NBC)
Newby, Paul   113–14
*New York Times*   88, 107
Nintendo   117
    *see also* video games

Packard-Bell   39
Palm-Mate   109–10, *110*, 111,
    112, 113
Parks, Lisa   60, 61
Parsons, Patrick R.   30, 32, 72
Patton, Doug   108, 109–10,
    *110*, 111, 116
pause   77, 114, 120
Peanut   113–17

Philco    16–18, *17,* 19, 29–30,
    *31,* 39
    Lazy-X    16–18, *17*
    Mystery Control
        29–30, *31*
Phonevision    34
Pioneer    97, 98
    Foresight 70    97
*Popular Mechanics*    6
*Popular Science Monthly*    22,
    27–9, *28*
PRM-1    108, *109*
pulse coding    80

radio    xii, xiv, xv, xvi, xviii,
    1–4, *2,* 5–32, 47
    amateur    5–6, *7*
    amplified sound    11–12
    audience    34
    Columaire    21–2
    commercials    24, 26
    consumption    8, 13–14, 17,
        20, 21, 25, 26, 30
    control    1, *2,* 12–13, *15,*
        22–3
    converters    14–15
    design    7–8, 9, 10–14, 20,
        21, 22–3, 27, 30
    domesticity    8–10, 12–13,
        16–17, 18
    K-45    1–4, *2,* 12, 14, 16
    Lazy-X    16–18, *17*
    leisure    9–10, *17*

luxury    16, 18, 23
marketing    11–14, 16–17,
    18, 21, 23–5
middle class    21
Mystery Control    29–30, *31*
programming    6–7
radio culture    3, 5–6, 23
281 remote    14–16, *15,* 23
soap operas    26
Telektor    12–14, *13,* 16,
    23, 82
volume    26–7
women    8–9, 10, 12–13,
    18, 19, 20, 26
Radio Act of 1927    5
*Radio Age*    6
Radio Aims at Remote Control
    (Lane)    27–9, *28*
Radio Corporation of America
    (RCA)    6, 7, 24, 39, 58,
    65–6, 70–1, *71,* 80, 94–7,
    *95,* 98
    Colortrak 2000    95
    Digital Command Center
        94–5, *95,* 96–7, 100
    Dimensia Digital Control
        94–7, *95,* 101, 114
    Magic Brain    39
    SJT400    95
    Wireless Wizard    65–6,
        71, *71*
radio culture    3, 5–6, 23
*Radio Digest*    25

RCA *see* Radio Corporation of
America (RCA)
RCA Victor *see* Radio
Corporation of
America (RCA)
*Reader's Digest* 40
Relyea, J. D. 27
281 remote 14–16, *15,* 23
Rizley, Ross 56, 58
RM-K1T 90, *91,* 108
RM V30 112, 113
RM-VP1 Remote Commander
111–13, 118
Roku 91, 123
Rothstein, Edward 107

Samsung 123, 124
Sarnoff, David 24
*Saturday Evening Post* 60
Sentinal 39
Servel 67
Electric Wonderbar 67
Silvertone 39
Medalist 39
SJT400 95
skeuomorphs 122–3
Smell-O-Vision 87
Son-R 56–8, *57*
Sony 76–9, *78,* 90, *91,* 97,
108, 111–13, 118, 123
Access 97
Betamax 76–8, *78*
RM-K1T 90, *91,* 108

RM V30 112, 113
RM-VP1 Remote
Commander 111–13,
118
STR-G1ES Vision Touch
112
Time Commander
77–9, *78*
Space Command 200 41,
54–6, *55,* 58, 60, 90, 113
Space Command 400 61–2,
*63,* 64, *65*
Spanish-American War xv
Spigel, Lynn 38
StarSight Telecast 117
STR-G1ES Vision Touch 112
Stromberg-Carlson 12–14,
*13,* 16, 23, 82
Telektor 12–14, *13,* 16,
23, 82
Swanson 67–9
TV Brand Dinners 67–9

TBS 73
Tech Master 39
Technics 97
AV500 97
Telektor 12–14, *13,* 16, 23, 82
television xi, xii, xviii, xix, 4,
32–42, 44–86, 87–124
accessories 66–9
Apple Remote 92, 119,
120–3, *121*

Apple TV   ix, xi, 92, 120–3

aspirational norm   44–5, 46, 59, 69–70, 85–6, 88

audience   34

Betamax   76–8, *78*

Blab-Off   39–41, 58

black box   92, 120–3

cable boxes   4, 81, 98

cable broadcasting   41, 47, 71–6, 81, 84, 117–18

celebrity endorsement   64–6, *65*

channel surfing   xix, 41, 43–4, 46, 72, 114–16, 118, 126

commercials   3, 5, 11, 23, 24–5, 26, 33–5, 39–41, 45, 49, 60, 62, 66, 73, 77, 86, 127–8

consumption   33, 41–2, 61, 67–9, 72, 82, 86

design   33, 39, 47–56, *48*, 66, 70–7, 79–81

Digital Command Center   94–5, *95*, 96–7, 100

Dimensia Digital Control   94–7, *95*, 101, 114

domesticity   38, 41, 44, 45–6, 48, 66–9, 76, 77, 82–4

DVD   87, 104, 119, 128

electronic program guides (EPGs)   43, 117–18, 119

entertainment centers   56, 82–4, 96, 98, 99

family dynamic   35, 37–8, 41, 64, 86

fast-forward   xiii, xiv, 77, 114, 116, 122, 128

Flash-Matic   41, 47–56, *48*, *50–1*, 79, 113

Fleetwood   39

gender roles   35, 36, 37, 47, 49, *50*, 52, 60–2, 64, 126

history   60–1

home theater   98–100, 112

home video   47, 76, 87, 119

Lazy Bones   33–9, *36*, 41, 64, 113

luxury   45, 62, 79, 86

Magic Brain   39

marketing   34–7, *36*, 40–1, 45–6, 49, 52, 58, 59–62, 64–6, *65*, 70, 77

Medalist   39

middle class   33

mute   xvii, 41, 53, 54

Palm-Mate   109–10, *110*, 111, 112, 113

patriarchy   35, 36–7

pause   77, 114, 120

pay-per-view   34

Peanut   113–17

Phonevision   34

PRM-1   108, *109*

rewind   77

RM-K1T   90, *91,* 108
RM-VP1 Remote
    Commander
    111–13, 118
Son-R   56–8, *57*
Space Command 200   41,
    54–6, *55,* 58, 60, 90, 113
Space Command 400
    61–2, *63,* 64, *65*
suburbanism   38
technology   33, 39, 45–6,
    47–56, 60, 61–2, 65–6,
    70–7, 79–81
television culture   xix, xx,
    41–2, 44–7, 59, 66–9
Telezoom   32–3, 41
Time Commander
    77–9, *78*
TiVo   113–17
Turret Tuner   35
TV dinners   67–9
VCR   76–8, 81, 84, 88,
    94, 95, 97, 98, 100,
    110–11, 116
video games   xviii, 83, 84,
    101, 116, 117, 128
Wireless Wizard   65–6,
    71, *71*
women   36, 37, 49, *50,* 52,
    60, 61, 64
television culture   xix, xx,
    41–2, 44–7, 59, 66–9
*Television Digest*   69

Television Twin   67
Telezoom   32–3, 41
Tesla, Nikola   xiv, xv
Texas Instruments   80
Time Commander   77–9, *78*
Time Inc.   73
Time Warner   117
TiVo   113–17
    Peanut   113–17
Toastmaster   67
    Television Twin   67
Turner, Ted   73
Turner Broadcasting System
    (TBS) *see* TBS
Turret Tuner   35
TV *see* television; television
    culture
TV Brand Dinners   67–9
TV dinners   67–9
TV Time Popcorn   69

United Video Satellite
    Group   117
Universal Electronic Atlas
    UCAP   *115*
Uppleva   84

VCR   76–8, 81, 84, 88, 94, 95,
    97, 98, 100, 110–11, 116
VCR-2   110–11
Veblen, Thorstein   13, 15
VHS   76, 77, 119
Viacom   117

video cassette recorder (VCR)
  *see* VCR
video games    xviii, 83, 84, 101,
    116, 117, 123, 128
Video Home System (VHS)
  *see* VHS
Viewstar    80
Virginia House    67

*Wall Street Journal*    43
WebTV    118
Westinghouse Electric
    and Manufacturing
    Company    21–2, 58
  Columaire    21–2
WGN Chicago    26
Wiley, Earl    126
Wiley, Paula    126
Winchell, Walter    40
Winston, Brian    71
*Wired*    109
*Wireless Age*    10
wireless telegraphy *see*
    amateur radio

Wireless Wizard    65–6, 71, *71*
World War I    xv
World War II    32, 33, 38, 49
Wozniak, Steve    101
Wright, Frank Lloyd    82, 127
  Hollyhock House    82

Xbox 360    128
  One    123
  *see also* video games

Zenith    33–9, *36*, 41, 47–56,
    *48, 50–1, 55*, 58, 61–2,
    *63*, 64–5, *65*, 79, 113
  Flash-Matic    41, 47–56, *48*,
    *50–1*, 79, 113
  Lazy Bones    33–9, *36*, 41,
    64, 113
  Phonevision    34
  Space Command 200    41,
    54–6, *55*, 58, 60, 90, 113
  Space Command 400
    61–2, *63*, 64, *65*
  Turret Tuner    35

| DATE DUE | | | |
|---|---|---|---|
| | | | |
| | | | |
| | | | |
| | | | |
| | | | |
| | | | |
| | | | |
| | | | |
| | | | |
| | | | |
| | | | |
| | | | |
| | | | |